Sandra L. Harris, Ph.D., series editor

Woodbine House ◆ 2005

Published in the United States of America by Woodbine House, Inc., 6510 Bells Mill Road, Bethesda, MD 20817. 800-843-7323. www.woodbinehouse.com

Library of Congress Cataloging-in-Publication Data

McClannahan, Lynn E.
Teaching conversation to children with autism : scripts and script fading / by Lynn E. McClannahan, and Patricia J. Krantz.
p. cm. -- (Topics in autism)
Includes bibliographical references and index.
ISBN-13: 978-1-890627-32-4
ISBN-10: 1-890627-32-1
1. Autistic children--Language. 2. Autistic children--Education. 3. Language arts. I. Krantz, Patricia J. II. Title. III. Series.
RJ506.A9M4263 2005
649'.154--dc22

2005011499

Manufactured in the United States of America

First edition

10 9 8 7 6 5 4 3 2

Honoring

Donald M. Baer

1931-2002

A founder of applied behavior analysis and

an advocate for children with autism.

Table of Contents

Preface

We stood in the hallway and watched the children begin another school day. All but the youngest carried their own book bags and most no longer needed help with removing coats or stowing lunchboxes in lockers. They looked very much like other youngsters, with one glaring exception—they didn't initiate conversation with teachers or peers. In fact, without verbal prompts from instructors, the morning routine would have been very, very quiet.

A seven-year-old approached us, and when his teacher, one step behind, prompted "Say 'Good morning,'" he quickly repeated the greeting, but did not wait for a reply.

We knew him and the other youngsters well, and our minimal prompts (saying "Hi," taking a step toward a student, or raising an eyebrow) resulted in greetings, but when we did not prompt, the children were silent, although virtually all of them had learned to talk. When imitating teachers' verbal models or answering questions, they responded with words, phrases, or sentences, but if they were not instructed to talk, they did not do so. Obviously, we had a problem.

The problem challenged us to ask questions, to reexamine intervention procedures for children with autism, and to undertake research. The solutions that we identified, documented, and put into practice are the topics of this book.

About This Book

This book focuses on the strategies we developed to help children with autism engage in the give and take of ordinary, daily conversation with parents, teachers, and peers. Our first investigation of the procedures we labeled "scripts and script fading" was published in 1993 and our research on this topic spans more than a decade.

The intervention strategies described in this book are based upon the science of applied behavior analysis. "Applied" means that the behavior studied is chosen because of its social importance. "Behavioral" refers to precise, reliable measurement that allows us to know whether behavior changed. "Analytic" means that we can demonstrate that the intervention procedures we used were responsible for behavior change (Baer, Wolf, & Risley, 1968). Because the social interaction skills of children with autism are critically important to their parents and teachers (and to us), we conducted research, carefully observed and measured their conversation, and demonstrated that increases in conversation occurred because of the teaching procedures we used.

Research shows that scripts and script-fading procedures have helped young people with diagnoses of *autistic disorder* and *pervasive developmental disorder–not otherwise specified* (American Psychiatric Association, 1994), and they have helped people who are more- and less-severely disabled. At the Princeton Child Development Institute, we have successfully used these procedures in the Early Intervention Program, in the preschool and school, in the adult program, in group homes, and in community settings. Parents of toddlers, children, and adolescents with autism have found scripts and script fading helpful in promoting conversation at home.

This book is intended for parents and professionals. The terms *parent, teacher, instructor,* and *therapist* are used interchangeably, because we believe that any educated person who is willing to invest sufficient time and effort can learn to use scripts and script-fading procedures to build young people's conversation skills.

It is important to note that scripts and script fading are not procedures for teaching children to *speak*, but procedures for teaching them to *interact*—to engage in the give-and-take of conversation. The strategies described in these pages help people with autism learn the nonverbal components of conversation (approaching and visually attending to another person), as well as the verbal components (initiating conversation, waiting quietly while others talk, and then responding to what they say).

Many parents and teachers know from experience that teaching children with autism to talk is no guarantee that they will engage in conversation. Youngsters who have acquired extensive spoken vocabularies and who have mastered the uses of adjectives and prepositions may never talk to parents about the events of the school day or initiate conversation with teachers about home activities. This book addresses those problems.

The length and complexity of conversation are related to vocabulary size. Babies' interactions with others often include nonverbal components of conversation, such as looking at another person and pointing or gesturing. Toddlers may interact with words or phrases, and school-age children carry on longer discussions. It is the same for children with autism: Youngsters who have not yet learned to talk can learn nonverbal interaction skills, children who have acquired only a few words can learn to use them to initiate conversation, and children who have larger vocabularies can learn to participate in longer social exchanges.

The table of contents provides a detailed outline of the topics covered in this book. Chapter 1 suggests some reasons that many children with autism do not learn to engage in conversation. Chapter 2 explains what we mean by "scripts" and "script fading."

Subsequent chapters describe how to use these procedures with young people who are at different language levels—from children who are not-yet-verbal to children who have learned to speak in sentences and paragraphs. The goal of these intervention procedures is to help children with autism learn to do more than say what we prompt them to say or answer our questions. The goal is to teach them to engage in real conversation with us.

1 Why Doesn't He Talk to Us?

Blake

Blake's home intervention began when he was three years old. His therapist came to his house for three hours every weekday, and they worked at a little table in the family room. Blake was asked to imitate words and phrases, answer questions such as "What's this?"; follow directions such as "Sit down" and "Look at me"; and point to various pictures and objects. His instructor gave him a sticker after each correct response, and he quickly learned to exchange the stickers for toys or small snacks. In only a few weeks, Blake also learned several other things: He learned not to leave his chair, make vocal noise, or grab toys or snacks while his therapist was getting ready for the next task. He learned to sit quietly and wait. Subsequently, his babbling diminished and he was increasingly skilled at waiting for his therapist to ask questions or give instructions.

Blake's therapist was a responsible young woman who earnestly prepared for his sessions, cared about him, and looked forward to working with him. She was pleased that when she asked, "What do you want?" he now requested a few foods and play materials with words or phrases ("cracker" or "want bubbles"). She was also pleased that he attempted to imitate more and more words, such as "dog," "hat," and "car," but she noticed that he never said these words during play activities unless she modeled them and instructed him to repeat them.

Blake learned many things that his therapist intended to teach, and some things that she did not intend to teach. For example, he learned to wait quietly. When he was quiet he received rewards, but if he vocalized he was not rewarded; therefore, vocalizing became less frequent, and there were fewer opportunities for his therapist and parents to reward spontaneous vocalizing that could be shaped into social interaction. Learning *when* to talk involves complex discriminations that may be difficult for typical children as well as for children with autism. It often takes a considerable length of time for typical preschoolers to learn that their parents enjoy talking to them during meals, playtime, car rides, and bath time, but not when they are talking on the telephone, conversing with adult guests, attending church, or paying for groceries. But children with autism, unlike their typical peers and siblings, often participate in thousands of highly structured teaching trials during which silent waiting is systematically rewarded, and many children seem to learn a rule: Talk only when asked (McClannahan & Krantz, 1997; Sundberg & Partington, 1999).

Learning to be quiet is only one of the problems that arise during intervention. Another difficulty is that the verbal exchanges that occur during discrete-trial teaching are not typical of ordinary conversation. For example, the instructor says, "What color?" The child replies "Red," the adult says, "Good, you said 'red,'" and the interaction ends.

Other language-training strategies, such as incidental teaching, present similar complications. For example, a youngster initiates by pointing to a toy telephone that is on a shelf beyond her reach. The teacher says, "What do you want? Say 'phone.'" The child says "Phone," and the teacher responds "Great, you said 'phone'; here's the telephone!" Exchanges of this type, which occur again and again, bear little resemblance to everyday conversation. Although these procedures may teach nouns, verbs, adjectives, and other parts of speech, they do not provide good models of the ways people usually talk to one another.

Other circumstances that interfere with the development of conversation skills may be related to the complex interplay of consequences that marks social exchanges between children with autism and their interaction partners; some of these patterns are present even in infancy. Most babies smile and coo when they are about to be picked up, held, or fed, but infants with autism who are passive and withdrawn are also picked up, cuddled, and fed, and the delivery of these important daily rewards immediately following social avoidance behavior may contribute to some babies' growing social isolation.

When parents of typical infants model simple verbal responses ("mmm, good," "oh-oh," or "all gone"), their babies often attempt to imitate those sounds or words, but when parents of babies with autism engage in such talk, their babies may ignore their verbal models. Gradually, over many weeks and months, parents may talk less and less when caring for their babies because of the infants' systematic failure to respond. Further, because most toddlers with autism have severe language deficits, their interaction with siblings may be confined to pushing, grabbing, or taking toys, with the result that young brothers and sisters increasingly avoid interacting with them. Grandparents and family friends who attempt to pick up and talk to young children with autism may discover that their efforts to communicate produce crying and struggling to escape and subsequently, their social overtures diminish. As a result, the youngsters have fewer and fewer models of social talk. These patterns of interaction between children with autism and those around them are often difficult to alter, and their persistence over time decreases children's opportunities to experience and learn about everyday conversation.

We wanted to help parents and teachers avoid these traps. Our research on scripts and script fading documented procedures that enable children to participate in interaction so that, like other youngsters, they are regularly exposed to others' talk and can make use of other people's language models in later conversation.

2 What Are Scripts? What Is Script Fading?

A script is an audiotaped or written word, phrase, or sentence that enables young people with autism to start or continue conversation. The audiotaped word "up" could be a script for a toddler; audiotaped sentences such as "I like trucks" and "Fire trucks are red" could be scripts for a preschooler with more language. A ten-year-old might read the typed scripts "I go swimming on Thursdays" and "Jan is my swimming teacher." The written script "I'm learning to shave" might be appropriate for a teenager, and an adult who has not acquired reading skills could use the audiotaped script "I work at a hotel."

The teaching procedures described in later chapters help people with autism learn to engage in social interaction. Scripts and script-fading procedures are useful to students who are more- and less-severely disabled, and to readers and nonreaders. Some important characteristics of scripts are that they can (and should) be individualized to take into account each young person's current language skills, his or her special interests, and the favorite conversation topics and special pursuits of family members and peers.

After a young person learns to imitate audiotaped scripts or to read written scripts, the scripts are faded by removing the last word, then the next-to-last word, and so on, until there are no words remaining. When faded, the audiotaped script "I like trucks" becomes "I like," then "I," and then a blank audiotape that has been erased. The written script "I'm learning to shave" is faded to "I'm learning to," "I'm learning," "I'm," and then a blank piece of paper.

And eventually, we also remove the blank audiotape or paper. At each step in the fading process, we observe whether a child or teen continues to say the script or uses words that have not yet been faded to create a new phrase or sentence. For example, when the script "I like trucks" is faded to "I like," some children continue to say "I like trucks," but others may produce new statements, such as "I like cars" or even "I like donuts." Later chapters provide more detail about how and when to fade scripts.

After many scripts have been presented and faded, most young people do one or more of the following:

1. they continue to say the scripts, although the scripts are absent;
2. they combine parts of the scripts with other scripts, or with language that was modeled by their conversation partners, thereby producing novel statements; or
3. they say things that were neither scripted nor modeled by their current conversation partners, but that were previously learned either via formal instruction or by imitating other people's conversation.

Suppose that a preschooler's audiotaped script is "want tickle," and her adult conversation partner often replies "Tickle your tummy." After the script is faded, the child may say a new, unscripted phrase, "Want tickle tummy." By combining the now-absent script with some of the language modeled by the adult, the youngster produces a novel phrase. Similarly, when a seven-year-old says the script "I like yogurt," the teacher often responds, "You like strawberry yogurt" or "You had yogurt for lunch." Later, when the script is absent, the student creates new sentences such as "I like strawberry yogurt" or "I like yogurt for lunch." More practice of conversation enables typical children to use more different words, and to develop larger vocabularies (Hart & Risley, 1999). Our data indicate that it is the same for youngsters with autism; the more they participate in social exchanges, the more likely they are to make novel statements.

Why do the young people continue to say the scripts after script fading begins? It is likely that they do so because of the formation of *behavior chains* (described by Bijou and Baer, 1965). In a behavior chain, each response produces a stimulus that reinforces that response and evokes the next response in the chain until (at least some of the time) a final reinforcer or reward occurs. When we learned to count, the words one, two, three, and four were initially discrete responses. There was a time when we could say "one, two," but not "one, two, three, four." But after we practiced, counting became a response chain in which saying the word "two" produced a stimulus that reinforced that response and evoked the word "three," and so on until we arrived at ten and a parent or teacher praised us saying, "Good for you—you counted to ten!" Similarly, for a youngster with autism, after the script "I can ride a bike" is mastered, each word evokes the next word in the sentence, and this continues to happen after words are faded so that, when encountering the partially faded script "I can ride," the child continues to say the entire sentence.

But we have also observed that, after many scripts have been learned and faded, students often stop saying the scripts. Instead, they combine parts of the scripts with language modeled by their conversation partners; or they combine parts of the scripts with language they learned in other contexts; or they combine parts of certain scripts with parts of other scripts; or sometimes, they say things we didn't teach, and that we didn't know they had learned!

3 Scripts, Script Fading, and Activity Schedules

When using scripts and script-fading procedures, an important goal is to enable people with autism to initiate conversation without being verbally prompted to do so, because, as noted earlier, verbal prompts ("Say 'Bye,'" "Tell Daddy 'I ate chicken,'" "Say 'I colored'") are not good models of conversation. In addition, such prompts may create prompt dependence, so that children or youths wait for others to give instructions or ask questions, rather than spontaneously engaging in social talk.

Activity schedules offer a way to circumvent these problems. An activity schedule is "a set of pictures or words that cues someone to engage in a sequence of activities" (McClannahan & Krantz, 1999). Three photographs—of a puzzle, a shape sorter, and a hobby horse—placed in a three-ring binder may cue a toddler to complete a frame-tray puzzle, put shapes in the shape sorter, and approach a parent for help with a ride on the hobby horse. A photographic activity schedule for a preschooler may cue him to put pegs in a peg board, complete a picture-matching task, build a tower of five large Lego™ blocks, say "Watch me" to a parent and receive help with a somersault, and eat a cookie. A written activity schedule for a beginning reader—for example, a three-ring binder with one or two words per page—may cue activities with words such as *bike, computer, book, talk,* and *snack*. And a written activity schedule for an older child may be a list of activities in a daily planner, such as *reading, math, talk, spelling, handwriting, talk, tell time, gym*, and *talk*.

Scripts and script fading are most effective when used in conjunction with activity schedules because activity schedules can be constructed in such a way that they remind children to interact with others. For example, an audio card (see Appendix A) attached to a page of a young child's activity schedule may cue her to remove the card from her schedule, run the card through a magnetic card reader to play the audiotaped script, and then approach a conversation partner and begin a conversation by saying the script. Or the word "talk" in an eleven-year-old's written activity schedule may remind him to remove a written script from a folder in his desk, approach a teacher, and initiate conversation.

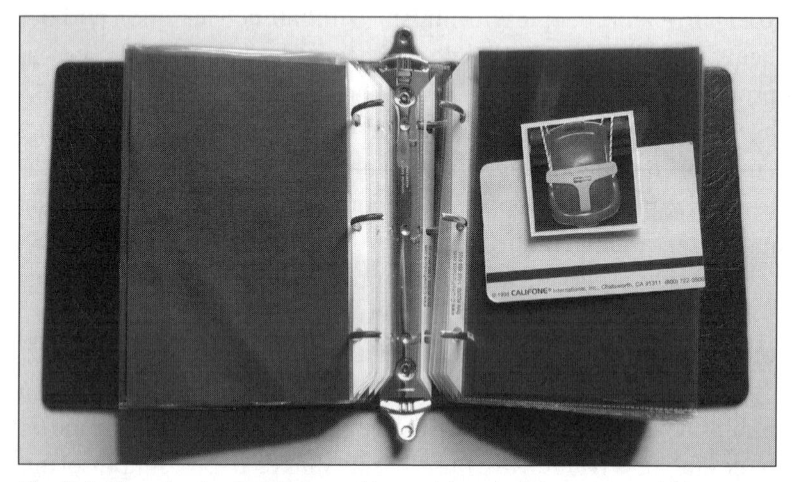

Fig. 3-1 Upon turning to this page of her activity schedule, a young child removes the audio card and the attached picture from her schedule, runs the card through the card reader to play the audiotaped script "swing," approaches her mother, and repeats the script. Her mother replies, "Sure, I'll swing you."

We teach children to use photographic activity schedules at the same time that we teach them to use first scripts. The prompting procedures used to teach children to follow activity schedules are similar to those used to help them learn to say scripts. Further, activity schedules offer a convenient way to sequence their activities, so that difficult social interaction tasks alternate with easier and more preferred activities. And when youngsters become more skilled at following activity schedules, many activities in their schedules provide topics for conversation. Scripts embedded in their schedules help them learn to talk about activities they have completed and those they are going to do.

Detailed descriptions of how to prepare photographic and written activity schedules and how to teach people to use them are presented in *Activity Schedules for Children with Autism* (McClannahan & Krantz, 1999). Subsequent chapters of this book also provide information about how to use activity schedules to cue conversation.

4 Building Prerequisite Skills: Scripts for Children Who Do Not Yet Talk

Allen

Allen's parents enrolled him in the early intervention program when he was twenty-six months old. Although he occasionally vocalized, he did not talk and did not imitate single sounds such as "mm" or "ah." He sometimes took adults' hands and pulled them toward objects—for example, he sometimes pulled his mother toward the refrigerator, or pulled his therapist toward a preferred toy—but he rarely looked at others. We noticed that he often laughed when sitting on the wagon or rocking on the hobby horse and he attempted to return to these activities when they ceased. Allen's first scripts were "juice," "wagon," and "horse." Because he couldn't yet talk, his scripts were audiotaped on cards. Each word was recorded on a separate card, a photograph of the object to which it referred was placed in a plastic baseball-card holder and mounted on the card, and Velcro™ was used to attach the cards to pages of his activity schedule.

Allen learned to remove a card from a page of his activity schedule, take it to a nearby card reader, and run the card through the machine to play the audiotaped word; a nearby instructor waited for him to orient toward her, confirmed his audiotaped request by smiling and saying "horse," "wagon," or "juice," and then quickly provided the requested activity. Allen practiced the sounds in these target words in separate, discrete-trial, verbal-imitation training sessions that taught him to imitate the sounds "ho," "wa," and "oo." Later, he began to say "ho" when he played the audiotaped script "horse," and "oo" when he played the audiotaped script "juice," although these vocal responses were never taught during the times that he used scripts.

Why Use Scripts with Nonverbal Children?

At first glance, Allen's scripts may not appear to resemble conversation, but consider that the "talk" of typical babies is often comprised of single sounds or words. For example, the mother points to the nearby family dog and says "Doggie, doggie," the child imitates, saying "Gog-ee," and the mother responds with attention and approval. Although Allen could not yet imitate others' verbal models, his audiotaped scripts enabled him to participate in social exchanges. The card reader (which he quickly learned to use) made it possible for him to produce audiotaped words that altered the behavior of others and gave him a measure of control over events that he enjoyed. During these "conversations," the scripts made it possible for his parents and teachers to avoid verbal prompts (such as, "Say 'wagon'") that are atypical of ordinary social interaction and that could create *prompt dependence*.

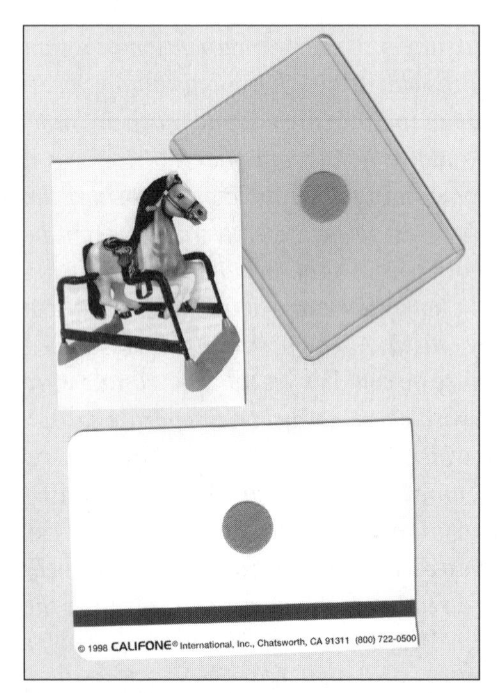

Fig. 4-1 A photograph of a hobby horse will be inserted into a plastic baseball-card holder, and attached with Velcro™ to a card with a magnetic strip that plays the prerecorded script "horse." The card was cut to more easily fit on a page of the child's activity schedule.

Card Readers

Card readers are audiotape recorders and players; they weigh four to six pounds, have carrying handles, and operate on household current or four "C" size batteries. Strips of magnetic tape are mounted on cards. To make a recording, an adult depresses the record button, inserts a card into the slot on the top of the machine, and speaks into a built-in microphone. When inserted on the right side of the machine, a card automatically travels through the slot from right to left, recording for approximately eight seconds. An erase-protection lock prevents accidental erasure. When children use card readers, they place cards in the slot and as the cards travel through the machine the audiotaped scripts are played.

Card readers are user-friendly devices. Even toddlers, whose fine-motor skills are not yet well-developed, learn to play scripts by putting cards in the slot. A special advantage of card readers (and other voice-recording mechanisms) is that they provide models of the prosody of speech—for example, variations in voice tone and the accents of syllables. Also, cards do not have to be "cued up" to the correct starting point, as do cassette tapes. See Chapter 5 for some considerations in preparing scripts on audio cards.

Making Social Interaction Fun

Allen's first scripts were selected because he showed interest in the things they represented—he frequently approached these objects, attempted to pull others toward them, and tried to continue the activities after they ended. Because we wanted him to learn to enjoy social interaction, we used these preferred activities as rewards for playing the audiotaped scripts, approaching an adult, and looking at a conversation partner.

Allen hadn't yet learned to use tokens, so we couldn't reward his correct responses with stickers, smile faces, or plastic "coins"; instead, we dropped one of his favorite snacks, Cheerios™, into a near-

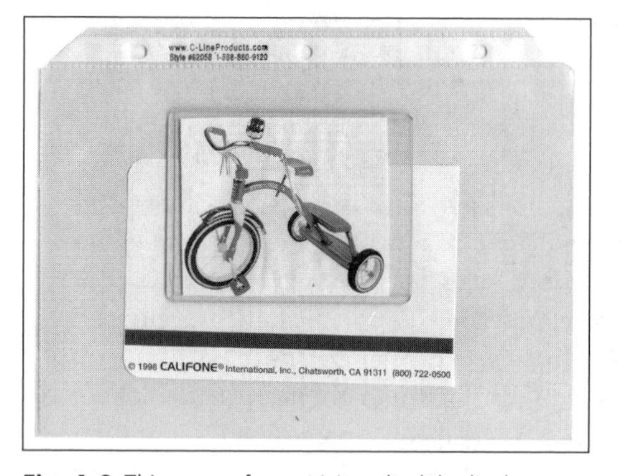

Fig. 4-2 This page of an activity schedule displays a picture of a tricycle attached to a card that plays the script "trike."

by, clear plastic cup immediately after he removed a card from his activity schedule, and after he turned to the audio card reader, and after he played the recorded script, and after he took a few steps toward the adult conversation partner and oriented toward her. Although hobby horse and wagon rides and drinks of juice appeared to be powerful rewards, it was also important to reward each separate response that preceded these activities. These new activities—obtaining and using the cards and approaching and orienting toward a conversation partner—were initially difficult for him; dropping Cheerios in the cup increased the frequency of rewards and provided feedback about correct versus incorrect responses. When teaching began, his instructor gave him the Cheerios after he completed each brief interaction. Later, when he was more proficient, he no longer needed this snack but continued to enjoy juice, hobby horse, and wagon rides.

Pairing Pictures, Words, and Objects or Activities

Like many other toddlers with autism, Allen had not yet learned that spoken words may refer to objects, nor had he learned that pictures represent objects. But when he engaged in a scripted interaction about the wagon, he saw the picture of the wagon that was mounted on the card, heard the word "wagon" when he played the audiotape, heard his conversation partner say "wagon" when he approached and looked at her, and saw the nearby wagon in which he was about to enjoy a ride. Through repeated pairings of pictures and words, followed by immediate access to preferred objects and events, Allen, like many other children, learned that words and pictures correspond to objects and activities.

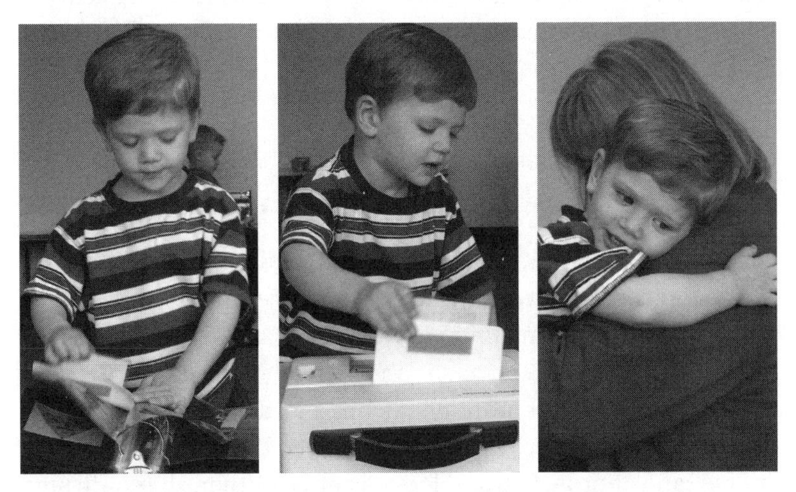

Fig. 4-3 Thirty-month-old Miles removes a card and attached photograph from his activity schedule *(left)*. He runs the card through the machine and hears the word "hug" *(middle)*. He approaches and orients toward his conversation partner who says "Here's a hug," and gives him an energetic hug *(right)*.

Some children do not acquire picture-object correspondence skills in this manner and need separate, discrete-trial training sessions in which the teacher displays a picture (for example, a picture of bubbles) and a few objects (perhaps bubbles, juice, and top). The teacher says "Point to bubbles" and if necessary, manually guides the child to point to the picture of bubbles. Then she says, "Find bubbles" and guides him to point to the object that corresponds to the picture. Correct responses (pointing to and finding bubbles) are rewarded by blowing bubbles. Similarly, pointing to a picture of the top and then pointing to the top is followed by spinning the top. Initially, only one picture and three objects are presented. Later, as the youngster gains skills, more objects may be added to the field of choices (e.g., a picture of a car, and four objects—car, ball, hat, and toy phone).

Some children's error patterns suggest that they are attempting to gain access to preferred items and activities rather than learning that pictures correspond to objects. If bubbles are a favorite activity, a child may consistently point to or reach for bubbles rather than selecting another object that corresponds to a picture. In this case, it may be helpful to reward correct responses with tokens or bites of food rather than with opportunities to play with the objects that correspond to the pictures.

Creating Helpful Language Environments

When Allen's first scripts were introduced, not only had he not yet learned that words like "juice" represent objects, he also had not learned the meaning of words such as "drink," "good," or "fun." Therefore, his conversation partner helped him by refraining from saying words he didn't understand, and by saying only the words in his three scripts. When he played the audiotaped script "horse" and approached and looked at his partner, she confirmed his initiation of interaction by saying "horse" in an enthusiastic voice tone, smiled at him, and quickly lifted him onto the hobby horse. By avoiding a cluttered language environment, she helped him attend to and learn the meaning of the target words. Later, as his vocabulary grew, she gradually added words to her conversation (e.g., "Juice—mm, good!").

We have known many young people with autism and only a miniscule proportion of them spent their early years in impoverished language environments such as orphanages. Most children have parents and siblings who talk to them, converse with one another, and model social interaction skills, but the youngsters are often unable to benefit from these experiences without special intervention. If you speak a second language, you may recall that when you first began to learn the new language you could understand a few slowly spoken and carefully articulated words, but mountains of discourse were not helpful. For many young people with autism, learning to talk and learning to engage in conversation are extraordinarily challenging. We can help them by remembering not to deluge them with words.

Not All Activities Are Social

Although social interaction skills are of special importance to people with autism, they are not the only skills to be mastered. Young children must also learn to play with toys; cooperate with mealtime, bathing, and bedtime routines; respond to simple instructions; imitate others' verbal and motor behavior; and do receptive language tasks ("Point to ____," "Give me ____," or "Come here"). Because social interaction tasks often appear to be the most difficult for youngsters with autism, and because we want them to enjoy conversation, the number and duration of such tasks must be carefully programmed. Massed practice of hard tasks may result in tantrums, task avoidance, and attempts to escape or avoid the people who present such tasks. It is helpful to alternate social and nonsocial activities. Playing with stacking cups, learning to complete a puzzle, learning to use the mouse to play a computer game, imitating gross motor responses presented on videotape, or sorting objects by color or shape may be welcome diversions after children attempt difficult interaction tasks.

5 Preparing to Teach

Teaching children with autism to engage in conversation requires some advance preparation. This chapter describes how to lay the groundwork for instruction.

Before instruction begins, parents or teachers prepare by:

1. Observing the child's preferences
2. Selecting the first scripts
3. Audiotaping the initial scripts
4. Enlisting the help of two adults who are available to participate in teaching the child to use scripts
5. Constructing an activity schedule that includes the scripts and a few other activities

Observe Preferences

The first step is to observe a child's preferences and identify toys, foods, or activities that he or she especially enjoys and that can be provided immediately after interaction episodes occur. These objects and events become the topics of conversation. Some children's preferences are obvious—they consistently reach for certain toys, pull adults toward favorite activities, or repeatedly request specific snacks. But if this is not the case, it may be helpful to present an array of toys, snacks, and activities and record which of them a youngster most often chooses (see Delmolino & Harris, 2004, for more information on assessing the preferences of children with developmental disabilities).

Select Scripts

If observation indicates that a youngster repeatedly selects tosses in the air, a fiber optic toy, and bites of banana, we may select these as beginning topics of conversation. Of course, scripts must be individualized to make them commensurate with children's language skills. If a boy does not yet speak, the words "up," "toy," and "banana" are recorded, and he initiates conversation by playing the audiotaped scripts. Later chapters describe how to create scripts for children who say sounds, words or phrases, or sentences.

Usually, scripts are taught in sets, because in ordinary conversation we do not discuss the same topic over and over—we talk about a variety of topics. For the same reason, we do not ask children to practice the same script over and over; we allow some time to elapse before the next practice. We do not talk about the weather and then talk about the weather, and we do not want to teach children to engage in repetitive interaction. The objective is to help them experience the social exchanges that are characteristic of ordinary conversation. Chapter 7 describes some additional considerations in selecting initial scripts.

Record the Scripts

When words are audiotaped on cards, it is helpful to avoid background noise, to articulate clearly, and to have the same person (a parent or familiar instructor) record the scripts, because children with severe language delays often have difficulty understanding different speakers. Later, when a youngster is more proficient, other adults may create audiotaped scripts.

It is also important to speak at a normal rate, or perhaps at a *slightly* slower speed, while preserving the normal tempo of speech. For example, when recording the word "book," we want to be sure that the vowel sound and both consonants are clear, but we don't want to elongate the model. We don't say "buh-ook" and we don't want to teach children to say that.

Enlist the Help of Two Adults

Initially, instruction for a child who is encountering his or her first sets of scripts requires the presence of two adults, one who serves as a prompter and another who takes the role of conversation partner. However, children's early conversations are quite brief and not very time-consuming. Parents sometimes schedule teaching activities before and after work, and teachers briefly enlist the assistance of their colleagues. Fortunately, the need for a two-to-one adult-child ratio is typically quite time-delimited; most children (even those with very severe disabilities) quickly learn to use a card reader and to approach and orient toward a conversation partner. They learn these skills because of very specific and well-defined prompting and prompt-fading strategies. One adult always remains behind the youngster and delivers prompts. The other, who serves as the conversation partner, does not use prompts at all.

Construct an Activity Schedule

Create a first activity schedule using a 7-by-9-inch binder such as the one shown in Figure 3-1. Three-ring binders are helpful because they lie flat when open. Insert pieces of black construction paper into five or six plastic page protectors, and put the page protectors in the binder. Then attach a Velcro dot to the center of each page.

Next, take photographs that represent the scripts and photographs that depict nonsocial activities. For example, if the scripts are "up," "toy," and "banana," take a photograph of a parent or instructor tossing the child in the air, a photograph of the favorite toy, and a photograph of a partially peeled banana and some bite-size slices. Then photograph some nonsocial activities—for example, a frame-tray puzzle, a shape sorter, and a preschool computer game. It is important to use photographs or very representational pictures from catalogs, rather than drawings or icons, so that children who have acquired picture-object correspondence skills can match each photograph to a depicted toy, snack, or activity. Many young children with autism may not yet have learned that drawings or icons represent objects or activities. Later, a generic picture of a swing set or a hobby horse may suffice, but initially, many children need photographs of the specific swing set or hobby horse that they use in their own home or school.

Place the photographs in clear plastic sleeves or clear plastic baseball card holders (available from hobby shops), and attach Velcro dots to the backs of the card holders. Attach the photographs of nonsocial activities to pages of the activity schedule, and attach photographs of social interaction activities to the associated audio cards. Then attach the cards to pages of the activity schedule. When turning to a page that displays a picture of a nonsocial activity, youngsters learn to point to the picture and then obtain the depicted materials. When turning to a page that displays a picture of a social activity, they learn to remove the picture and the audio card from the schedule and run the card through the card reader to play the script.

Sequence the photographs so that social and nonsocial activities alternate. Which depicted activity is the child's favorite? Place it in the final position in the schedule.

6 Teaching Children to Use Scripts: Prompters and Conversation Partners

The two adults who help children learn to engage in conversation have very different roles. The prompter's job is to prevent errors whenever possible. But errors sometimes occur, and then it is important to help a youngster practice correct responses. The conversation partner, on the other hand, does not prompt, ask questions, or give instructions; instead he or she looks interested in the child, enthusiastically responds to the child's initiations, and helps the youngster enjoy the toy, snack, or activity that was the topic of conversation.

How to Be an Effective Prompter

When teaching first audiotaped scripts to a young child, materials such as activity schedule and card reader are placed within the child's easy reach on a desk or coffee table, and the conversation partner is nearby (perhaps three feet away, sitting on the floor or on a little chair in order to be near the child's eye level). Most children progress more rapidly if initial instruction occurs in the same place each time—for example, in the family room or in the same corner of the classroom.

The adult who is the prompter stands behind the youngster and uses *manual guidance*, or hand-over-hand prompts to help him open his activity schedule or turn a page, remove an audio card and the attached photograph from his schedule, turn to the card reader, and run the card through the machine to play the audiotaped script. Manual prompts to the child's shoulders are used to guide him to approach and orient toward the conversation partner. Manual prompts to the head and neck are not used because they may not be well tolerated, resulting in crying, disruptive behavior, or attempts to escape.

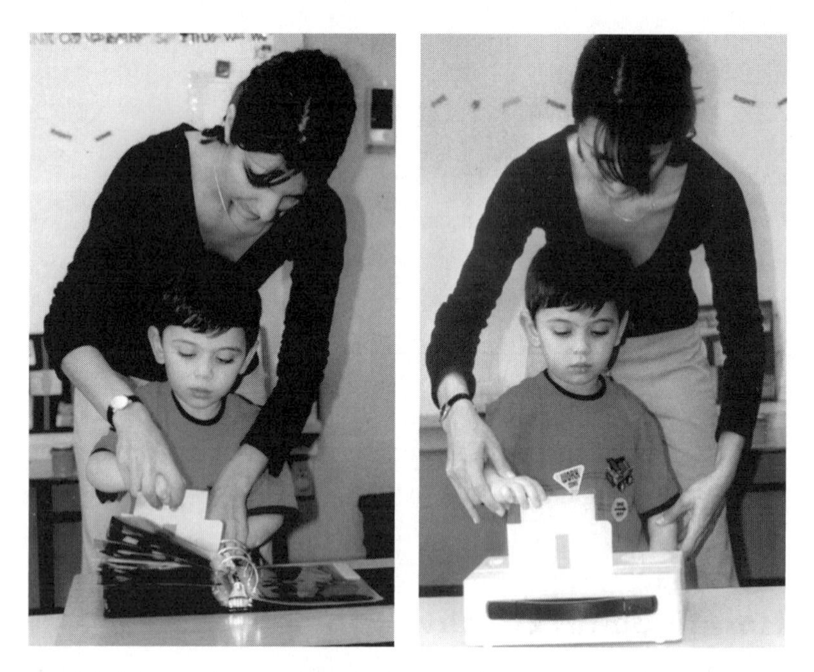

Fig. 6-1 The prompter manually guides Kent, age 3, to remove a card and a photograph from his activity schedule book *(left)*. Manual guidance is also used to help him run the card through the card reader, which plays the audiotaped word "spider" *(right)*. When Kent approaches and orients toward his conversation partner, she says, "Spider!" and then sings "The Itsy Bitsy Spider," one of his favorite songs.

The skillful use of manual guidance prevents most errors, so that most children quickly acquire relevant skills, especially if each response in the response chain is immediately rewarded. After some practice, prompters learn not only to use manual guidance, but also to deliver rewards (from behind the child) by putting bites of a favorite snack in a toddler's mouth, dropping bites of preferred snack foods into a preschooler's cup, or placing tokens on a token board. Initially, correct responses are rewarded even if they are prompted; later, only correct, unprompted behavior is followed by rewards.

Prompters should be as "invisible" as possible, because they are not participants in conversation. They should be careful not to put their hands, arms, or any parts of their bodies between children and their materials, or between children and their conversation partners, because this may interfere with the development of independent performance.

Fading Prompts

As a youngster displays increasing competence, the adult begins to fade manual prompts by using *graduated guidance*; although the prompter's hands continue to be placed over the child's hands or on the child's shoulders, less guidance is given. Typically, this procedure provides useful feedback to parents and teachers. On the basis of the learner's hand, arm, and body movements, the adult can quickly determine whether the next response will be correct or incorrect, and can prevent errors by guiding, or promote independence by allowing correct responses to be completed with less assistance.

When children complete all of the component tasks with minimal guidance, the prompter uses *spatial fading* (Cooper, 1987). That is, prompts in the form of light touches are initially delivered on a child's hands, and are gradually moved from her hands to her forearms, then to her elbow or upper arm, then to her shoulder or back. But if an error occurs, the adult returns to the previous prompting procedure—in this case, graduated guidance—until the child makes several correct responses.

Spatial fading is followed by *shadowing*. That is, the prompter's hands follow the child's movements, but without touching her. At first, the adult may shadow as closely as six inches from the child but if her responses are correct, the prompter gradually increases the distance to one foot, eighteen inches, and so on.

When the adult shadows and the youngster makes no errors, it is time to *decrease proximity*. For very young children, this may mean that the adult gradually moves three feet away, then four feet, then five feet, and so on. For some children, it is possible to gradually decrease proximity until the prompter is on the other side of an activity area, or just outside the nearest doorway.

The Many Tasks of the Prompter

1. Remain behind the child and do not speak to him or her.
2. Deliver rewards (drop snacks in a cup, deliver tokens).
3. Use manual guidance to prevent errors.
4. Begin prompt fading by using graduated guidance.
5. Then use spatial fading (light touches on a youngster's hands, forearms, shoulders, and back).
6. Next, shadow the youngster.
7. Then decrease proximity—gradually move farther away.
8. When an error occurs, return to the prior prompting procedure and conduct a behavioral rehearsal.
9. As quickly as possible, stop rewarding prompted responses and reward only correct, unprompted responses.
10. Conduct behavioral rehearsals if inappropriate behavior (crying, stereotypy, running away) occurs.

The progression from graduated guidance to spatial fading to shadowing to decreased proximity is a prompt-fading sequence. Careful prompt fading enables a child to initiate social interaction by independently approaching and orienting toward a recipient of conversation. But if the learner makes an error, the adult immediately returns to the prior prompting procedure. This helps to prevent additional errors and increases the likelihood that the child will receive rewards for her next responses.

When a child is learning a first set of scripts, it may be helpful to have the same adult serve as prompter. Later, when the youngster is familiar with the teaching procedures, other adults may be invited to prompt.

How to Be a Good Conversation Partner

As discussed above, discrete-trial training does not usually offer good examples of the give-and-take of ordinary conversation. Scripts and script-fading procedures are useful in helping young people with autism gain experience with more conventional social exchanges. In order to accomplish this, adult conversation partners model language that is at, or only slightly above the learner's language level, and that we hope is of interest to the child. As noted previously, initial scripts are based almost exclusively on children's observed preferences for various activities and materials, and these early scripts enable children to gain immediate access to preferred items or events. That is, the scripts function as requests because this helps to make social interaction rewarding.

It is very important that the adult conversation partner does not give instructions or ask questions, because this quickly transforms the interaction from a conversation to a discrete-trial training session, with the associated problems of prompt dependence described

The Many Tasks of the Conversation Partner

1. Invite interaction by looking at and smiling at the child.
2. Respond enthusiastically to the youngster's attempts at conversation.
3. Ensure a language environment that is representative of the youngster's language level—use words that are likely to be understood.
4. Make conversation as "natural" as possible.
5. Make interesting comments.
6. Model appropriate voice volume and intonation.
7. Model gestures—for example, pointing when making a statement such as "I like *that* one," or using expansive hand movements when commenting about big objects.
8. Provide powerful rewards for social interaction by delivering the preferred activities, toys, or snacks that were the topic of the child's initiation.

in Chapter 1. And although it's helpful to praise frequently during discrete-trial teaching, behavior-specific praise ("Good talking" or "Good, you looked") isn't representative of typical conversation.

Being a good conversation partner isn't as easy as one might imagine, but we adults have as many opportunities to practice as the youngsters who are learning to use scripts. After some experience with the role of conversation partner, many parents and instructors perform it flawlessly.

Dealing with Errors

Young children commonly make errors such as not removing an audio card from the activity schedule, not running the card through the card reader in such a way that the audiotaped script is played, not approaching the conversation partner, and not orienting toward the conversation partner. Initially, manual guidance prevents many of these errors, but when prompt fading begins, errors may be more frequent.

When an error occurs, the adult prompter immediately returns to the previous prompting procedure, and also helps the youngster complete a *behavioral rehearsal*. For example, if the child did not correctly play the audiotaped script, or did not orient toward the conversation partner, the prompter returns the card to the child's activity schedule and prompts her to repeat the entire sequence—remove the card from the schedule, move to the card reader, play the audiotaped script, and approach and orient toward the interaction partner. Rehearsals continue until the target responses are correctly completed. It is important to note that the prompter does not talk to the child or use verbal prompts ("Next time, remember to look at Mom"), because we want to help the child focus on the conversation partner, who will still be present after the prompter's proximity is faded.

The prompter also returns to the previous prompting procedure and conducts behavioral rehearsals if a child engages in inappropriate behavior such as hand flapping or hitting. Suppose that while the prompter is using spatial fading and lightly touching the child's shoulder to prompt her to approach her conversation partner, the youngster suddenly attempts to dart away. The prompter now returns to graduated guidance, using just the amount of guidance necessary to help the child return to her activity schedule and complete a behavioral rehearsal. But if she again attempts to leave the area, the prompter uses full manual guidance to ensure that she will correctly complete the next behavioral rehearsal. It is also important to prompt when children do not respond quickly, because delays are often followed by errors or inappropriate behavior.

Initially, correct prompted responses that occur during behavioral rehearsals are accepted and immediately rewarded, but when youngsters become more proficient, behavioral rehearsals are repeated as many times as necessary until the relevant responses are correctly completed *without* prompts, and only then are rewards given. When conducting behavioral rehearsals, it is important to prompt children to repeat the entire response sequence. If rehearsals begin in the middle of the sequence—for example, rehearsing only the behavior that pertains to approaching and orienting toward the conversation partner—some children may learn that they need not always obtain cards and play the recordings.

Measuring Progress

When scripts are used with children who are not-yet-verbal, the goals are to teach youngsters:

1. to remove pre-recorded cards from the pages of activity schedules,
2. to run cards through the card reader in such a way that audiotaped scripts are correctly played, and
3. to approach within three feet of a conversation partner and orient toward him or her.

These first responses are important to future skill development, and we want children to master them before more complex tasks are presented. Data on a child's performance tell us when to present new tasks.

Because the adult who serves as prompter is typically very busy using graduated guidance, spatial fading, or shadowing, and delivering rewards, the conversation partner usually assumes data-collection responsibilities. The data collector scores plus (+) if the child correctly completes the target response without assistance and without displaying any disruptive behavior (such as crying, falling to the floor, attempting to hit or bite, or engaging in repetitive behavior such as hand flapping). Minus (-) is scored if the youngster does not begin a response within five seconds, incorrectly performs the response, is prompted, or engages in inappropriate behavior (see Figure 6-2). Chapter 17 offers strategies for preventing and managing inappropriate behavior.

Fig. 6-2 Data Sheet

Sample data sheet used to measure the progress of a child who is not-yet-verbal. (A blank Data Sheet is in Appendix B.)

Child: Allen **Observer:** Mom **Date:** Feb. 6, 2005 **Script Set:** 1

Script #	Get card from schedule	Play audiotape	Approaches and orients
1	+	+	-
2	+	+	+
3	+	-	+
4			
5			

Response definitions

[a] Removes audio card from a page of the activity schedule

[b] Runs card through card reader and correctly plays audiotape

[c] Approaches to within 3 feet of conversation partner and orients toward him or her

Script 1 Horse

Script 2 Wagon

Script 3 Juice

Script 4

Script 5

It is difficult to monitor progress by examining data sheets; they soon accumulate and review is increasingly difficult. Figure 6-3 displays a Daily Individual Progress Report chart that may be used to summarize the data on correct responses and errors. The chart shows that Allen's errors were scattered, but most were scored because he did not approach and orient to his conversation partner. When he used Script 1 (horse), orienting to his partner was scored incorrect on six days; he made three such errors on Script 2 (wagon), and three more on Script 3 (juice). With additional practice, his errors decreased. The data show that during the last four days, he made only one error, and was ready for his therapist to introduce some new scripts.

Fig. 6-3 Daily Individual Progress Report

Sample data summary for a child who is not-yet-verbal.
(A blank Daily Individual Progress Report is in Appendix C.)

Child: Allen **Correct=** ■ **Incorrect=** □ **Script Set:** 1

Notes							Mom & Dad agreed all correct			Changed order of scripts
5c Orients										
5b Plays audiotape										
5a Gets card										
4c Orients										
4b Plays audiotape										
4a Gets Card										
3c Orients	■	□	■	□	■	□	■	■	■	■
3b Plays audiotape	□	■	■	■	■	■	■	■	■	■
3a Gets card	■	■	■	■	■	■	■	■	■	■
2c Orients	■	□	□	□	■	■	■	■	■	■
2b Plays audiotape	■	■	■	■	□	■	■	■	■	■
2a Gets Card	■	■	■	□	■	■	■	■	■	■
1c Orients	□	□	□	■	□	□	■	□	■	■
1b Plays audiotape	■	■	■	□	■	■	■	■	■	■
1a Gets card	■	■	□	■	□	■	■	■	■	■
Year: 2005 Date:	2/6	2/7	2/8	2/10	2/11	2/12	2/15	2/16	2/17	2/19

Response definitions
[a] Removes audio card from a page of the activity schedule
[b] Runs card through card reader and correctly plays audiotape
[c] Approaches to within 3 feet of conversation partner and orients toward him or her

Script 1 Horse
Script 2 Wagon
Script 3 Juice
Script 4
Script 5

Collecting data on children's performance makes it possible to individualize intervention decisions and determine whether more practice is needed or whether it is time to present new challenges. Some children's performance stabilizes after only a few sessions and their errors become infrequent. Other children need many weeks (or even months) of teaching before they master the relevant skills. If youngsters display consistent error patterns or make many scattered errors that do not decrease over time, it is important for prompters to return to full manual guidance for several sessions before again fading prompts, and the prompt-fading sequence may need to be repeated several times.

What's Next?

During the initial steps in teaching young children who do not yet talk, prompts are faded but scripts are not. After a youngster masters one or two sets of scripts, it is often helpful to put the scripts in a different order in the activity schedule, and to present the scripts at different times of day, in different rooms at home or different settings at school, and to introduce new conversation partners. However, during this early stage of instruction, adult conversation partners are preferable because they are willing to wait patiently, smile in an encouraging way, visually attend in a manner that invites interaction, and respond enthusiastically with words that they hope the child will understand. These responses are often difficult for siblings and peers.

Of course, changes in the ways that scripts are presented must be made sequentially. When the data show that a child consistently responds to task variations, it is time to introduce new scripts which, after they are mastered, should also be rotated across time, settings, positions in the activity schedule, and conversation partners.

7 Scripts for Children Who Say Words or Phrases

Gary

When Gary was enrolled in the Early Intervention Program, he had no speech and he seldom babbled. Because he smiled when rocking on the seesaw or when pushed in the chair swing, his instructors frequently provided these activities, and they soon noticed that when the seesaw or the swing stopped, he sometimes vocalized. These observations were important because they suggested procedures to increase babbling. Many opportunities to swing and rock on the seesaw were interspersed with other learning activities, and swinging and rocking were often intentionally interrupted. His teachers stopped, waited, and looked expectantly at him, and when he vocalized they quickly resumed the activity. In less than a month, these procedures produced increases in Gary's babbling, and his instructors observed that the sounds "ee" and "buh" were very frequent, although he did not imitate these sounds when they were modeled by others.

In verbal-imitation sessions, Gary's instructors modeled the sounds "ee" and "buh" and rewarded his efforts to approximate their models by providing favorite toys and snacks. Initially, they helped him imitate by gently pushing the corners of his mouth into a "smile" position when they modeled "ee," and by gently holding his lips together and quickly releasing them when he attempted to say "buh"; these manual prompts were discontinued when his imitation skills improved. As soon as adults could readily distinguish Gary's production of "ee" from his production of "buh," a third sound ("ah") was introduced. It was selected not only because it was occasionally heard when he babbled, but also because it was possible to use a manual prompt (applying gentle, downward pressure to his chin) to help him open his mouth to correctly imitate this sound.

Now it was time to make Gary's speech sounds meaningful. His teachers observed his choices of toys, activities, and snacks, and after reviewing his preferences they decided that "ee" would represent the word eat, "buh" would be used as an approximation to bubbles, and "ah" would be accepted as the word "on" (which would mean "turn on the videotape"). After these decisions were made, his first scripts were recorded on audio cards, and pictures of snacks, bubbles, and TV were attached to the relevant cards.

But before Gary was ready to say the three scripts, some additional teaching was necessary: An instructor manually guided him to play a card by running it through the card reader and waited for him to imitate the target word—and was not surprised when he did not. In subsequent discrete-trial sessions, his instructors manually guided him to play the audiotaped scripts "eat," "bubbles," and "on," then quickly modeled the target sounds that he could say ("ee," "buh," and "ah"), and rewarded his imitative responses. Next, while continuing to use graduated guidance to help Gary play the audiotaped scripts, the instructors gradually decreased their voice volume until they no longer vocalized the target sounds, and he began to make those sounds after the audio cards were played. Now, he was ready for his first experiences with scripts.

Gary learned to remove the cards from his activity schedule, move to the card reader that was located on the same little desk, play an audiotaped word, approach and orient toward a nearby conversation partner, and approximate the word on the audiotape. When he played the script "eat" and approached an adult and said "ee," the adult smiled, enthusiastically confirmed, "Eat," put him on her lap, and offered one of his preferred snacks. When he played the script "bubbles" and said "buh," his conversation partner took his hand and said "Bubbles," and quickly blew bubbles that he attempted to catch. And when he played the script "on," and said the approximation "ah," his interaction partner said "on," put him on her lap and turned on his favorite videotape.

Gary's imitation of the audiotaped scripts became increasingly accurate. After several weeks of practice, he surprised and delighted his interaction partner by playing a script, approaching her, and saying something that sounded very much like "bubbles."

Initiating Conversation with a Word or Phrase

When children with autism learn to say words, our expectations change. Now they must not only go to the card reader and play an audiotaped script, but they must also say the script (or an approximation of the script). A toddler who has learned to say a few words has scripts such as "up," "go," and "pop"; when he says these words to his mother, she confirms these initiations with one or two words ("up high," "go out," "lollipop"), picks him up and tosses him in the air, or helps him go out to the back yard for a quick walk or a chasing game, or helps him lick a lollipop. Other examples of one-word scripts are "book," "swing," "ride" (trike, wagon, or piggy back); "play" (with a favorite toy); and "TV," "car," "ball," "tickle," and "cup." Scripts are selected because a youngster can say the target words, which, although they may not be perfectly articulated, are understood by those who know him. And as noted earlier, scripts are also chosen because the objects or activities they represent are preferred by the child.

When children learn to say phrases, they may have scripts such as "want up," "play horsie," or "tickle me." Other scripts enlist adults' assistance; for example, a card with the audiotaped script "help me" may be accompanied by a picture of a special toy that is kept on a high shelf, beyond a little girl's reach. She plays the audiotaped script, approaches an adult, and repeats the script "help me," and her interaction partner makes a brief reply ("Sure, I'll help") and obtains the requested toy. Or the audiotaped script "open please" is paired with a picture of a favorite snack in a transparent plastic jar with a tightly closed lid, so that saying the script "open please" results in the reply, "I'll open it," and assistance in opening the container. Of course, if children do not say the scripts, behavioral rehearsals are conducted until the target responses are independently displayed.

Both parents and professionals often make very accurate observations about the words children do and do not understand.

When a girl learns to say one-word scripts, her father may decide to make small, careful changes in his responses. For example, when she approaches him and says "ride," instead of merely confirming by saying "ride," he may say "ride trike," or "go ride trike." But it is important not to ask questions ("Where's your trike?" or "What do you want to ride?"), and not to give directions ("Go find your coat," or "Come with me"). Questions and directions transform the activity from conversation to instruction, and defeat the purposes of scripts and script-fading procedures.

When a child masters one or two sets of three scripts, you may decide to add one or two new scripts to each set, and then to again rotate the scripts across different positions in the activity schedule. Next, you may move the card reader farther from the youngster's activity schedule, and then increase the distance between the card reader and the conversation partner. These changes must be gradual; if the conversation partner moves three additional feet from the card reader and the child does not say the scripts, the conversation partner returns to her original location. When the youngster again correctly says the scripts, the distance between card

Suggestions for Constructing Scripts

1. Choose words or phrases that will enable the child to gain immediate access to preferred objects and activities.
2. Use words that the child understands.
3. Select scripts that begin with different words, because when scripts are faded, different first words may promote more varied conversation. If all of the scripts begin with the same word (for example, "I did math," "I did spelling," "I did reading") some children may say only one or a few scripts after all of the fading steps are completed.
4. Attempt to use good grammar, even though articles, pronouns, prepositions, or other parts of speech may be omitted to keep the scripts short, or because the child can't yet say them or doesn't yet understand them.
5. Make scripts age appropriate. Young children may say "bow wow" or "doggie," but kindergarteners say "dog."

reader and conversation partner is increased in small increments (perhaps one foot at a time) after one or two sessions in which the youngster correctly says the scripts.

An Additional Measure of Progress

Performance measurement now expands to include data on children's verbal initiations. We continue to record data on whether a youngster removes a card from his schedule, plays the audiotape, and approaches and orients toward an adult, but in addition we record whether he says the script. "Saying the script" means that he repeats each word on the audiotape (although words may be imperfectly articulated). Figure 7-1 displays a data sheet that was

Fig. 7-1 Data Sheet

Sample data sheet used to measure the progress of a child who says words or phrases. (A blank Data Sheet is in Appendix D.)

Child: John **Observer:** Eleanor **Date:** May 21, 2005 **Script Set:** 8

Script #	Get card from schedule	Play audiotape	Approaches and orients	Says script
1	+	+	+	+
2	+	+	-	-
3	+	+	+	+
4	+	+	+	-
5	+	-	+	-

Response definitions
[a] Removes audio card from a page of the activity schedule
[b] Runs card through card reader and correctly plays audiotape
[c] Approaches to within 3 feet of conversation partner and orients toward him or her
[d] Says the word or words on the script

Script 1 want up
Script 2 play horsie
Script 3 tickle me
Script 4 open please
Script 5 help me

used to track the developing skills of three-year-old John. In Sets 1 through 4 (not shown), he learned to play audiotaped scripts to initiate conversation, although he did not yet say the scripts. In Sets 5 through 7 (also not shown), he said one-word scripts to his interaction partners. With the introduction of Set 8, shown in Figure 7-1 on the previous page, he began learning to say two-word scripts.

John's data summary sheet (the Daily Individual Progress Report shown in Figure 7-2) was revised to include the new task—saying the script. His instructor continued to summarize

Fig. 7-2 Daily Individual Progress Report

Sample data summary for a child who says words or phrases.
(A blank Daily Individual Progress Report is in Appendix E.)

Child: John **Correct=** ▒ **Incorrect=** ☐ **Script Set:** 8

Notes								Partner moves 3 feet farther away		Prompter is now 3 ft distant
5d Says script										
5c Orients										
5b Plays audiotape										
5a Gets card										
4d Says script										
4c Orients										
4b Plays audiotape										
4a Gets Card										
3d Says script										
3c Orients										
3b Plays audiotape										
3a Gets card										
2d Says script										
2c Orients										
2b Plays audiotape										
2a Gets Card										
1d Says script										
1c Orients										
1b Plays audiotape										
1a Gets card										
Year: 2005 Date:	5/27	5/28	5/29	5/30	6/2	6/3	6/5	6/6	6/10	6/11

Response definitions
[a] Removes audio card from a page of the activity schedule
[b] Runs card through card reader and correctly plays audiotape
[c] Approaches to within 3 feet of conversation partner and orients toward him or her
[d] Says the word or words on the script

Script 1 want up
Script 2 play horsie
Script 3 tickle me
Script 4 open please
Script 5 help me

the data on his performance and to review his errors, most of which were related to saying the new scripts. Prompts were seldom necessary when he was obtaining a card, running it through the card reader, or approaching and looking at an adult. Figure 7-2 shows that after June 5, when John made only one error, his conversation partner moved farther away from him. Then, after two consecutive data-collection opportunities when he correctly completed all of the target responses, the prompter also began to move farther away from him.

It is usually possible for one adult to assume the roles of prompter and conversation partner when:

1. the data show that a child is making only a small number of errors and that errors are scattered rather than related to specific task components,
2. most prompts have been faded, and
3. a youngster receives a reward only after independently completing all four of the target responses relevant to each script.

Acting as both prompter and conversation partner requires some practice, because when prompts are necessary they must continue to be delivered from behind the child. For example, if a boy incorrectly runs a card through the card reader, producing garbled playback, the adult quickly moves behind him and prompts him to return to his schedule, uses the minimal prompting procedure necessary to help him correctly obtain and play the card, and takes her place as conversation partner before he moves toward her chair. Of course, the adult who plays these dual roles is also responsible for rewarding correct performance.

What If a Child Doesn't Say the Scripts?

If a boy plays an audiotaped script and approaches and orients toward a conversation partner but does not say the script, the audio card is returned to his activity schedule and a behavioral rehearsal occurs. If he again approaches his interaction partner and does not say the script, behavioral rehearsals continue until he does so; *verbal prompts and models are not used*. It is important to teach children to consistently say the scripts before script fading begins. If a youngster does not say a script after several behavioral rehearsals, it is often helpful to resume rewarding each separate response in the response chain (that is, reward him for removing the card from the schedule, for playing the audiotaped script, and for approaching the adult). The frequency of rewards is gradually diminished after he makes several correct, unprompted responses.

It may also be helpful to simplify the tasks. You may experiment with decreasing the distance between the card reader and the conversation partner or increasing the volume at which the audiotape is played. If the script is more than one word, it may be useful to temporarily return to a single word (for example, by deleting the audiotaped "open please" and recording the word "open"). And it's always a good idea to attend to the quality of the audiotapes; cards that are worn, bent, or dirty should be replaced. Typically, some combination of these strategies is effective in helping a child learn to say the scripts. But imitating audiotaped models is very difficult for some children and it is occasionally necessary to provide additional discrete-trial verbal-imitation training (see Lovaas, 2003) to help children develop additional imitation skills. In the interim, young learners may continue to use audiotaped scripts to initiate conversation, as described in Chapter 6, but it is important to separate discrete-trial teaching from instruction about using scripts.

Fading Audiotaped Scripts

When the data show that a child has learned to say audiotaped scripts, script fading begins. The data permit us to make individualized decisions about when to fade the scripts. Some children quickly learn to say the scripts and make virtually no errors; some make occasional errors; and some continue to make one or a few errors on each set of scripts, even after many practice opportunities. Continued, scattered errors may indicate that although a youngster has learned to use scripts, he has not yet learned to pay sustained attention to these (and other) tasks. As a general rule, we begin script fading:

1. if a child's error rate is low and stable,
2. if he is not making the same errors consistently, and
3. if he is dependably saying two-word phrases.

We begin script fading by removing the last word of each phrase. New audio cards that play only the first word of each script are placed in his activity schedule and photographs of the relevant objects or activities continue to be attached to the cards.

When youngsters encounter their first script-fading experiences, they often do not say the scripts at all, or say only the parts of the scripts that remain. When this occurs, the previously described prompts and prompt-fading procedures are used, with one exception. If a boy does not say the partially faded script after two or three behavioral rehearsals, the new card is replaced by the old one, and the complete script is played. But as soon as he again says the script, the original card is removed and the card with the partially faded script is returned to his schedule. This process continues until the youngster says the complete two-word script when the last word is no longer present. These procedures enable parents and teachers to avoid the verbal prompts that often create prompt dependence and prevent the emergence of conversation skills.

When a child consistently says the scripts after the last words are faded, the remaining words are removed from each audiotape and the pictures of toys, snacks, or activities are attached to blank cards. It is interesting to note that when children first encounter blank cards, some respond by playing the cards again and again and some repeatedly push the buttons of the card reader, as we might do when contending with a piece of equipment that is not in working order. We allow these responses to continue until the youngster approaches and says the script or starts to make an error (for example, returning to the activity schedule or leaving the area). In the latter case, the adult quickly prompts the child to run the blank card through the card reader and approach the conversation partner. If this prompt does not enable the child to say the script after several behavioral rehearsals, then we return to a card that plays the partially faded script and when the youngster dependably responds, we reintroduce the blank card.

After children learn to approach adults and say words or phrases in the absence of audiotaped scripts, we assess their developing skills by removing the blank cards, but the pictures that were previously attached to the cards remain in their activity schedules as cues for social interaction. Some youngsters continue to respond to the photographs by approaching adults and saying the now-absent scripts; we then add new scripts that will continue to expand their conversational repertoires. Other children no longer say the scripts when blank cards are removed. Sometimes, alternately presenting and removing the blank cards results in conversation in the absence of the cards, but if this does not occur we assume that more practice is needed before a young person can engage in unscripted conversation and we move on to the next set of scripts.

8 Measuring Scripted and Unscripted Interaction

Kip

When he entered intervention at the Princeton Child Development Institute at twenty-three months of age, Kip had no functional speech. By the age of three, he had learned to imitate many sounds and words and had mastered several sets of one-word scripts, but he only initiated conversation when he encountered photographs attached to blank audio cards in his activity schedule, and his initiations were confined to scripts that were previously faded.

Kip's first set of two-word scripts was based on one of his favorite preschool picture books. The five target phrases in this set were "look book," "hot dog," "duck quack," "a baby," and "yummy chips." Five scripts seemed to be an appropriate number that would keep the activity relatively brief and maintain his attention. He learned to remove the first card (with an attached photograph of the preferred book) from his activity schedule, play the audiotaped script "look, book," approach his conversation partner, show her the picture of the book, and say the script. His partner made a brief, conversational reply ("Good book!") and placed the book and the card reader on a little desk that displayed the four remaining cards and attached photos of objects in the picture book.

Kip and his interaction partner turned the pages of the book, and she occasionally pointed to pictures and made brief statements that she judged Kip might understand, such as "Look, spoon," or "Cat says meow." When they arrived at a page that displayed a picture relevant to one of Kip's scripts, she waited five seconds to give him an opportunity to play that script; if he did not, she prompted him to run the card through the card reader and then waited for him to orient toward her and say the script.

Kip quickly learned to say two-word scripts about the pictures in his favorite book. He also began to display some proprietary behavior about his audio cards. For example, after he removed cards from the card reader, he carefully put them in a nearby container provided for that purpose; if a card fell to the floor, he picked it up and returned it to its proper location; and if he said a script and his partner did not respond because she was interacting with another student, he said his script again.

New Definitions of Interaction

When children are learning to use scripted words and phrases as "conversation starters," we listen very carefully to what they say, because the emergence of unprompted and unscripted language is a sign that we should begin to observe and measure additional responses. We now define *interaction* as one or more understandable words that are said when a youngster is within three feet of a conversation partner, is oriented toward her, and is not prompted to approach, orient, or speak. If a child interacts in this way, but then repeats the same word or phrase, or echoes a conversation partner's statement, these repetitions are not counted as interaction. And responses to an adult's questions or instructions are also not scored as interaction because, as noted earlier, giving directions and asking questions make the activity less like conversation and more like discrete-trial training (Krantz & McClannahan, 1998). All of these requirements apply to both scripted and unscripted interaction.

Scripted interaction is defined as saying the script when all or part of the audiotaped script is present. If a child says the script "duck, quack" when the audiotape is partially faded to "duck," that phrase is scored as scripted.

Unscripted interaction is defined as saying one or more understandable words in the absence of a script or portion of a script. If a child says the script "look, book" when the script is completely faded and the card is blank, that statement is scored as unscripted. If a girl says "look, cookie" after the script "look, book" is completely faded, that is scored as unscripted. If a boy plays the audiotaped script "hot dog" and says "yummy chips," that phrase is also counted as unscripted. Or, best of all, if a child plays a blank card and says "Mama" (which was never part of a script), that word is scored as unscripted.

At this early stage of language development, most children with autism have not yet learned about staying on topic and do not have sufficiently large vocabularies to do so. For these reasons, understandable words—on any topic—are scored as unscripted if they are said in the absence of a script.

Observing, Scoring, and Graphing Scripted and Unscripted Interaction

When children begin to say words or phrases, every teaching session offers opportunities to play and say each script, and parents or teachers score each of these opportunities. Recording a plus (+) sign on the data sheet indicates that the youngster said the entire script without prompts; recording a minus (-) sign signifies that she did not say the script, said only part of the script, or was prompted (for example, a parent used graduated guidance or shadowing, or conducted a behavioral rehearsal). Because young children with autism do not usually speak quickly, frequently, or at length, unscripted statements are recorded verbatim. That is, observers write unscripted words, phrases, sentences, or questions word for word, in the order in which the child says them.

Figure 8-1 on the next page shows a data sheet for Kip. On this day (June 5, 2004), he correctly said all five scripts, and also said one unscripted phrase—"The end." After collecting these data, his teacher totaled the number of scripted and unscripted statements, and added these data points to his graph (see Figure 8-2). Note that the left side of the graph is numbered by twos, from two

Fig. 8-1 Data Sheet

Sample data sheet used to score scripted and unscripted interaction.
(A blank Data Sheet is in Appendix F.)

Child: Kip **Observer:** Courtney **Date:** June 5, 2004 **Script Set:** 7

Scripted Interaction	Correct (+)	Incorrect (-)
Script 1: Look, book	+	

Unscripted Interaction

Scripted Interaction	Correct (+)	Incorrect (-)
Script 2: Hot dog	+	

Unscripted Interaction

Scripted Interaction	Correct (+)	Incorrect (-)
Script 3: Duck, quack	+	

Unscripted Interaction

Scripted Interaction	Correct (+)	Incorrect (-)
Script 4: A baby	+	

Unscripted Interaction

Scripted Interaction	Correct (+)	Incorrect (-)
Script 5: Yummy chips	+	

Unscripted Interaction

The end

Number of correct scripted statements 5

Number of unscripted statements 1

to ten, and the bottom of the graph shows the dates on which data were collected. (One can avoid entering calendar days on graphs by purchasing *six months by days* graph paper; it is already divided into months, and days of the month are numbered).

On Kip's graph, the number of scripted statements that he said each day is represented by closed circles, and a solid, horizontal line indicates that he had five scripts. Number of unscripted statements is represented by open circles; the first open circle appears on Kip's graph on June 5—it was the first unscripted phrase that was recorded.

Figure 8-2 on the next page also shows that when the last words of Kip's two-word scripts were faded on April 30, he did not say any of them; subsequently the original scripts were restored, and on the following day, he said two of the five scripts, although the last words were absent. On May 8, 9, and 12, he said all of the scripts when only the first word of each script was present. But on May 13, when he encountered blank audio cards, he said only three of the five scripts, and several days passed before he again said all of the scripts. After audio cards were removed, Kip's teacher was very pleased that he continued to say three to five of the five scripts and on June 5 she was elated when, after closing the book, he said, "The end," a phrase she had often modeled. "The end" was the first unscripted statement recorded, and she quickly provided several special rewards—she tossed him in the air, added extra snacks to his cup, enthusiastically confirmed his unscripted response ("Right—it's the end!"), and provided an immediate opportunity for him to play with his favorite toys. For several days, Kip either said no unscripted statements or occasionally said "the end," but on June 17 he again surprised his teacher by saying, "Look, chips" (a combination of the first and fifth scripts in Set 7) before he said, "The end."

When the first unscripted statements occur, it is important to provide special and immediate rewards and it is best to do this in the context of the conversation. When Kip said, "Look, chips" his teacher replied, "Chips are good!" and dropped extra snacks in his cup. If he had said, "The end" before the end of the book, she might have said, "It's almost the end," and rewarded him. Although children's early attempts at conversation are not always accurate, we do not want to punish their efforts. Continued practice and additional language models provided by their conversation partners will build their interaction repertoires.

Fig. 8-2 Number of Scripted & Unscripted Statements Graph

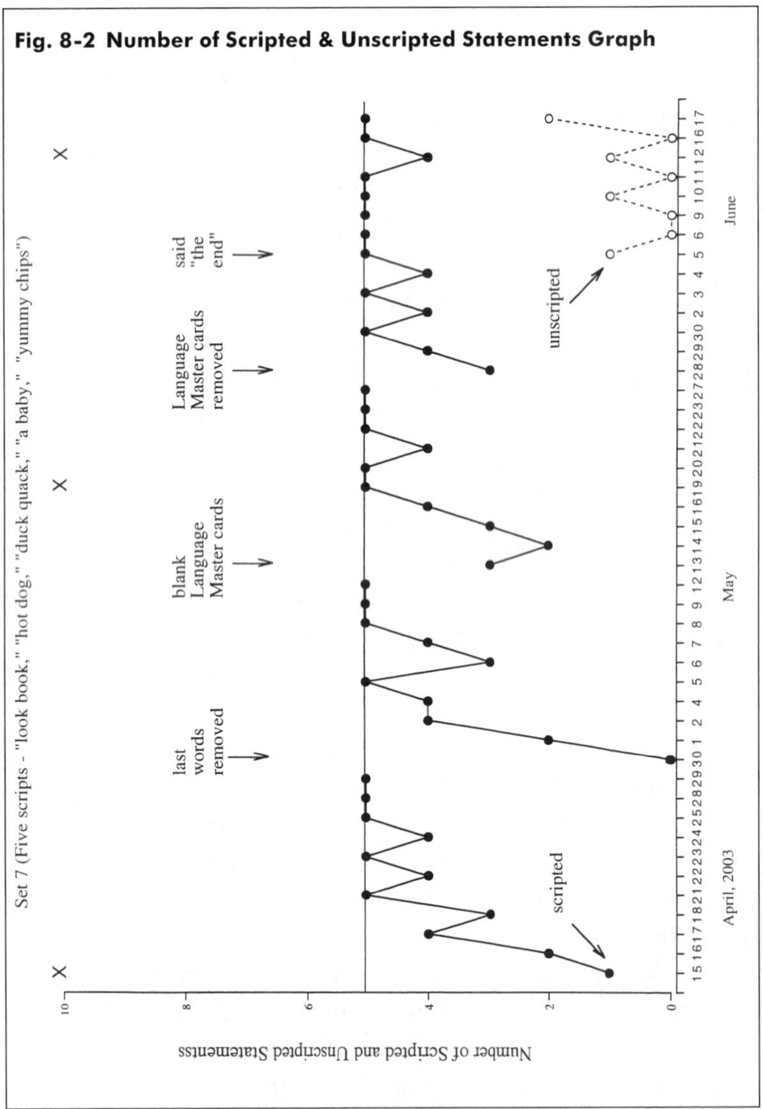

The Importance of Two Observers

Because we care about young people with autism, and because we are invested in their progress, it is easy to lose objectivity about their current skills and skill deficits. But if our measures of scripted and unscripted statements are not good representations of a child's attempts at conversation, then our graphs are meaningless. This is problematic because if the data are not believable, they are not useful in making decisions about when to fade scripts, add new scripts, or introduce new teaching procedures. For these reasons, we sometimes ask two data collectors to obtain *interobserver agreement*—that is, to independently record data on the same target responses at the same time and to assess their agreement with one another.

Independent observers should stand where they will have equally good views of the child, but should be unable to see one another's data sheets and should not interact with one another during data-collection activities. In practice, we assume that if two independent observers agree with one another on at least four-fifths or 80 percent of their observations, we can have reasonable confidence in the data. If they agree on less than 80 percent of observations, it is often helpful to:

1. review the definitions of scripted and unscripted interaction;
2. discuss the observers' reasons for scoring or not scoring specific responses;
3. reevaluate whether their locations provide both observers with unobstructed views of the youngster; and
4. reconsider whether they are equally adept at understanding a child's (often low-volume and poorly articulated) words and phrases.

The term "mother's ear" acknowledges that those persons who spend the most time with young children are often most skilled in understanding their talk. Differences in "mother's ear" that result in low interobserver agreement scores can often be remedied if the observer who is less familiar with the child's speech spends some additional time listening to the youngster during other types of language-training sessions, such as incidental teaching or discrete-trial teaching.

To assess interobserver agreement, two observers do an item-by-item comparison of their data sheets. Agreements on saying a script are scored if both observers marked that script plus or both marked it minus. If one observer marked plus and the other marked minus, or if one observer did not record, a disagreement is noted. Agreements on unscripted statements are assessed by comparing each successive recording on the data sheet. For example, if both observers wrote "the end" in the unscripted interaction section that follows Script 5 (see Figure 8-1), an agreement would be scored. A disagreement would be scored if one wrote "the end" and the other wrote nothing, or if one wrote "the end" and the other wrote "pretend."

It is helpful to keep a record of interobserver agreement between the primary (or usual) data collector and secondary (or occasional) observers. Kip's teacher marked an "X" at the top of his graph to indicate each day when interobserver agreement was obtained (see Figure 8-2); her colleagues collected data with her on April 15, May 19, and June 12. On the back of the graph, she wrote:

Date	Agreement on Unscripted Statements	Agreement on Unscripted Statements
4/15/04	4/5	
5/19/04	5/5	
6/12/04	5/5	1/1

Her record shows that on April 15, she and another observer agreed on whether Kip said four scripts, and they had one disagreement; neither observer recorded any unscripted statements. On June 12, they agreed that he said all five of the five scripts, and they also agreed that he said one unscripted statement.

9 More Scripts and More Interaction Opportunities

Trevor

Toilet training began a few days after Trevor's third birthday. His diapers were exchanged for training pants, and a kitchen timer was set for thirty minutes. When the timer sounded, a therapist took him to the potty, gave him a book to look at, sat nearby and waited for five minutes, and rewarded his successful uses of the potty with preferred toys and activities. But in addition to these aspects of his toilet-training program, his instructors also took a photograph of the potty, attached it to a small, button-activated recorder called a Mini-Me (see Figure 9-1), and placed the picture and recorder near his activity schedule. When the timer rang, an instructor or parent manually guided him to point to the picture of the potty and press the button to play the script "I want potty."

Trevor had previously learned to use a card reader, approach adults, and say scripts, and he quickly learned to respond to the ringing timer by pressing the button of the miniature recorder to play the script and then turn to a therapist and say "I want potty." She confirmed his initiation by saying, "Okay, let's go potty," and they immediately went to a nearby bathroom. Subsequently, the script was faded to "I want," and then "I"; then the script was absent. A short time later the button-activated recorder was removed, but the picture of the potty remained on his desk, near his activity schedule.

When successful uses of the potty increased and toilet accidents decreased, the timer was set for longer periods of time—first forty-five minutes, then an hour, then ninety minutes. Usually, when the timer signaled, Trevor continued to point to the picture of the potty and turn to his instructor and say, "I want potty" but if he did not, he was manually guided to point to the picture, and this prompt enabled him to say the now-absent script.

A few months later, Trevor no longer had accidents during preschool, but he did not spontaneously request the potty. Therefore, his instructors set the timer for varying intervals, and when it rang (three times each morning), he continued to point to the photograph and say "I want potty." Next, the timer was set for only two unpredictable times each morning and then only once each morning (except that, on occasions when Trevor's squirming and grabbing his pants suggested that a trip to the potty was necessary, his teachers quickly made the timer ring). Not long after this, he squirmed in his chair and held the front of his pants, but before an instructor could make the timer ring, he volunteered, "I want potty." Subsequently, he began to request bathroom trips in the absence of the timer signal. But the picture of the potty remained on his desk for some time, as a reminder to request trips to the bathroom.

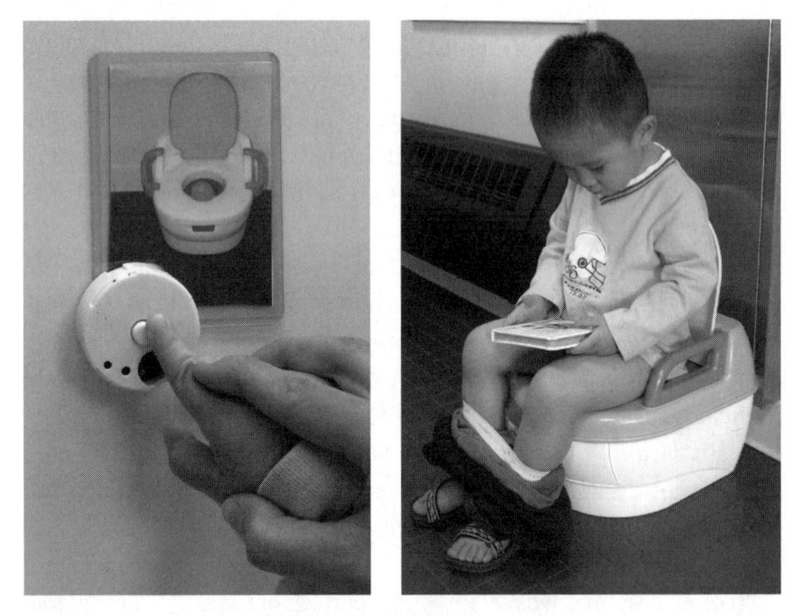

Fig. 9-1 A button-activated recorder was attached to a picture of a potty. When Trevor pressed the button to play the script "I want potty" and then said the script, his therapist quickly took him to the bathroom. Later, the script was faded and he learned to spontaneously request the bathroom.

In a high-tech world, many applications of technology prove useful for people with disabilities. For example, scripts can be recorded and played on card readers, talking picture frames, and greeting cards. Button-activated voice recorders such as the Mini-Me™ and the Voice-Over™ (see Appendix G) can serve special purposes because of their small size and portability. In general, we first teach children to use card readers, and later to use button-activated recorders. This chapter describes some of the uses of button-activated recorders.

Talking about Reward Activities

Children practice new responses and develop new skills because teachers and parents repeatedly reward their best efforts and their correct responses. We work hard to identify snacks, toys, and activities that each youngster prefers and to find new rewards that will promote learning. And as quickly as possible, we teach children to choose rewards from an array of several possible items or activities. Because selecting a reward is typically a high-interest activity, it is an opportune time to build social interaction skills.

After a young child learns to use scripts recorded on cards or on button-activated recorders, we teach him to use scripts to select rewards. Three to five favorite snacks or special toys are displayed, each in a clear container with a tightly closed lid, with Mini-Mes mounted on the lids. In response to a picture of the containers in his activity schedule, the child approaches the shelf where they are displayed, chooses a container (or is manually guided to do so), presses a button on a Mini-Me (or is guided to do so), hears a recorded script such as "candy" or "want candy" or "candy, please," and repeats that script. The teacher makes a brief, conversational reply ("Mm, candy is good!"), waits with her hand poised above the container until the youngster visually attends to her, and then quickly removes the lid and provides the requested item.

Or, after earning a specified number of tokens, a girl exchanges them for an opportunity to choose among items displayed on a shelf. Mini-Mes are attached to the shelf, below clear plastic boxes that contain puzzles, Lincoln Logs, cars, blocks, and books. The youngster selects a box that contains cars, plays the recorded script "play cars," and turns to the nearby instructor and says the script. The instructor says, "Cars are fun!" and sits down on the floor to participate in the play activity.

Choices of reward activities may also be displayed on easels, bulletin boards, or foam boards that are placed within children's reach. For example, photographs of a wagon, a trike, a video cassette, a see-saw, a computer, and a piggy-back ride are attached with Velcro™ to a display board, and Mini-Mes are attached to each photograph. After earning all of his tokens, a preschooler approaches the board and reviews his choices, removes the picture of the computer, and goes to his teacher and activates the recorder to play the script "I like computer." His instructor responds, "Let's play the coloring game," and they go to the computer. Of course, when children dependably say the audiotaped scripts, the scripts are faded from last word to first word, then the Mini-Mes do not play any scripts when activated, and then they are removed and a new set of scripts is presented. Parents and teachers use the previously described prompting procedures and behavioral rehearsals to prevent and correct errors.

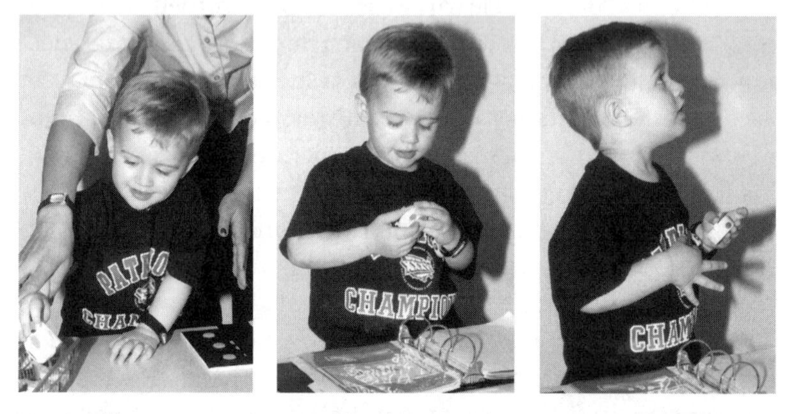

Fig. 9-2 Vance, age three, is manually guided to obtain a Mini-Me. He presses the button to play the recorded script "Let's do words" and says that script. His instructor replies, "Words are fun" and gives him a token. When he responds with the unscripted statement, "Like words," she quickly gives him two tokens and says, "You learned the word 'big.'"

Talking about Play Activities

Many children with autism must be taught how to play with toys, and most do not talk while using play materials. Scripts and script-fading procedures are useful in helping youngsters learn to talk during play. To teach young children to talk while playing with farm animals, we take photographs of the animals and attach a button-activated voice recorder to each photograph. The toy animals are placed near the matching photographs. When a toddler picks up a cow, he is manually guided to activate the recorded script "moo" and say the script, and the adult replies, "Cow says 'moo'" and helps him put the cow in the barn. When he reaches for the sheep, he plays and says the script "baa," and the adult says, "Sheep says 'baa,'" and helps him put the sheep inside the fence.

Similarly, in the kitchen area of our preschool, scripts recorded on nearby Mini-Mes may include "stove on," "cook burger," "all done," "get plate," and "let's eat." Button-activated recorders near a dollhouse play scripts such as "here's mommy," "feed baby," "get dog," "go upstairs," and "night-night," and scripts that accompany toy cars and trucks include "big truck," "beep, beep," "stop," "go fast," and "crash." Initially, parents and instructors not only manually guide children to play the scripts, but also use graduated guidance (and later, spatial fading, shadowing, and decreased proximity) to teach them to appropriately use toys.

Miniature voice recorders such as Mini-Mes and Voice-Overs are also helpful in teaching children to talk about outdoor play activities. A Voice-Over attached to the bottom step of the slide plays the script "Watch me slide," one on a strut of the swing set plays the script "I like to swing," and one in the garage where the bike is stored plays the script "I ride fast."

In all of these activities, children continue to be rewarded with snacks or tokens when they say scripted and unscripted statements, but the reward choices, toys, and play activities also function as rewards. Correctly using button-activated recorders, saying scripts, and engaging in unscripted conversation result in immediate access to toys and play activities, and errors result in behavioral rehearsals that delay access to those rewards.

As youngsters' vocabularies and conversational repertoires expand, they may no longer need photographs attached to audio cards or button-activated recorders. After the last words in a set of recorded scripts are faded, we may remove the associated pictures and then the recorders. The data on scripted and unscripted statements will reveal whether the photographs and recorders are still useful.

Card Reader Versus Button-Activated Recorder

Button-activated recorders are more portable than card readers, but "wear out" more quickly (the batteries die or recording quality diminishes). They also require isolation of a finger (a "pointing response") in order to depress the buttons. They are especially useful because, thanks to their small size, they can be mounted on a variety of objects, such as light switches, cookie jars, door frames, computer monitors, tricycles, bookcases, car seats, and many different types of toys. After scripts are faded and the recorders are removed, the objects themselves may be the cues for interaction, so that children's conversation, like our own, is evoked by features of their environments.

Both card readers and button-activated recorders play scripts of approximately the same length, but card readers may have better fidelity. Also, when children learn to say five sentence-length scripts on a specific topic, a card reader and five cards may be more convenient than an array of five button-activated recorders.

Talking about Home-Living Activities

Miniature voice-recorders, strategically placed around the home, are helpful in cueing children to interact with family members. A Mini-Me mounted on the door jam enables a child to say "I'm home!" when returning from school. When a boy accompanies his mother to the basement to play nearby while she does the laundry, he activates a Mini-Me near the top of the stairs and says the script, "Going down." In the kitchen, he opens a cupboard door, presses a button, and repeats the script "Can I have a cookie?" A Mini-Me on a bathroom shelf may play a script such as "wash hands," "brush teeth," or "take a bath." And a Mini-Me on a nightstand may cue a youngster to say "Give me a hug" or "I love you."

Patrick

Because seven-year-old Patrick is an experienced user of audiotaped scripts, photographs are no longer attached to his Mini-Mes. When he consistently said the scripts after they were faded, the photographs were removed. Initially, he stopped saying the scripts in the absence of the photos, and they were replaced. When he resumed saying the scripts, the pictures were removed again, and this process was repeated several times until he learned to say the scripts in the absence of the photographs.

Patrick still needs supervision when dressing for school. He approaches the dresser in his bedroom, activates the Mini-Me on top of the dresser, turns to his mother and says the script "I'm getting dressed." She replies, "Good for you!" and pauses briefly. When he says the unscripted word "dresser," a word she has used in previous conversations, she quickly adds a token to his token board. After he earns all ten tokens for completing dressing and hygiene activities, he exchanges them for television time until his school bus arrives.

His mother helps him acquire dressing skills by arranging items of clothing in sequence in top-to-bottom dresser drawers. When he opens the top drawer, he plays the script "Get underpants." The Mini-Me in the second drawer plays the script "Put shirt on," and the one in the third drawer plays "Put pants on." Each of these scripted statements is followed by a brief but enthusiastic response from his mother and the delivery of a token. Recently, Patrick consistently said all of the scripts about his morning preparations for school and the last word of each script was faded. He also said several unscripted phrases that were novel combinations of his mother's comments and his scripts, such as "Get shirt" and "Put socks on."

Patrick's mother has already identified the next set of scripts she will introduce after these scripts are faded. They will include "Wash face," "Brush teeth," and "Hang towel."

Extending Conversation

In this chapter, we gave examples of scripts that are one to five words in length (e.g., "candy," "feed baby," "cars are fun," "I like to swing," and "Can I have a cookie?"). Gradually lengthening the scripts is a way to extend the child's side of the conversation. Decisions about the length of scripts are based on a youngster's current language skills. If he dependably says two-word scripts after they are faded, we may foster additional language by introducing three-word scripts. But scripts are also selected because a child can pronounce or approximate the pronunciation of the words in each script, and because we believe or have data to demonstrate that he understands most of the words in target scripts. For example, if scripts pertain to farm animals, we can determine whether he understands those words by asking him to "Point to cow" or "Give me sheep," but we do not do these discrete-trial activities when the youngster is using scripts.

Adult interaction partners extend their conversation in two ways. First, when children say longer scripts, adults provide slightly longer replies. If the child's script is "cookie," the adult may reply "Good cookie!" but if the child's script is "Can I have a cookie?" the adult may say "Yes, here's a chocolate cookie." The adult should not say, "Yes, I just got these cookies at the bakery; they were baked fresh this morning," unless she is sure that the youngster understands words such as "bakery," "fresh," and "morning."

Secondly, adults extend conversation when children begin to say unscripted statements, because each of a child's contributions to conversation is acknowledged with a reply. If a child who is playing with the farm set says the script "moo," the adult replies, "Cow says 'moo.'" But if the youngster then says an unscripted word such as "horse," the adult might say, "Horse is walking," while moving the horse toward the barn. Or if, at bathtime, a child says the script "take a bath," the adult replies "Bathtub is fun"; if the child then says the unscripted phrase "Fun bubbles," the adult responds "Put bubbles in the tub."

Conversation partners should *not* extend conversation by minimally rephrasing children's statements, tempting as that is (for example "You *did* take a bath" or "Bubbles *are* fun"). Rephrasing statements makes it more difficult for children to make unscripted replies. Because we do not want children to echo our statements, we should refrain from echoing theirs. On the other hand, for young children, children with minimal language, and children who are just beginning to use scripts, hearing an adult make the same reply each time a child says a script may help him or her learn and later use that comment (for example, each time a toddler says "moo" the adult replies, "Cow says moo").

During children's early efforts to learn social talk, adults reply to each of their statements but the children determine when conversation ends. When an adult responds to a child's last word,

A Note about Speech Intelligibility

The utterances of children with autism (and typical children) are sometimes unintelligible. They have difficulty with pronunciation, they engage in vocal experimentation, and they "make up" words. When we are teaching conversation, we never respond to a child's unintelligible speech with instructions or questions. Instead, we make conversational replies, such as "I couldn't hear you," "That sounds like (the word ____)," or "Talking is fun," or we return to the topic of the most recent script. For example, if the script was "take a bath," the adult might reply to garbled speech with a comment such as "Here's your boat" or "Nice warm water" or "Lots of bubbles." More practice with conversation will help to alleviate these problems. There are times when all of us say things that others do not understand.

phrase, or sentence, pauses, and the child adds nothing more, conversation is over until the youngster says the next script or makes another unscripted statement. This is an important rule, because interaction tasks are difficult for youngsters with autism, and lengthy conversations may be punishing. And of course, adult conversation partners never ask questions or give instructions.

When Are Scripts Faded?

How does one know when to fade scripts? Should scripts be faded after one day on which a learner says all of the scripts? Should he say all of the scripts for three consecutive sessions? Should we fade the scripts when he consistently says four of five scripts? These questions are best answered by referring to the data on a child's scripted and unscripted statements. After each fading step, some children dependably continue to say the scripts, some make errors but resume saying the scripts after only a few sessions, and some recover their previous performances only after we return to a prior fading step and conduct many behavioral rehearsals.

The question of when to fade scripts is important because if we wait too long, we waste valuable time during which a child could master many more scripts and combine those words with words modeled by his conversation partners to create novel statements. On the other hand, if we fade scripts too quickly, we generate errors that require us to respond with prompts and behavioral rehearsals that may make social interaction less enjoyable.

Data on a youngster's first sets of scripts help us decide when to fade. The data in Figure 8-2 (Chapter 8) show that five days after the last words of Kip's scripts were removed, he said all of the scripts, but on the next two days he made errors. Because his instructor had noted a similar pattern in the data on his previous sets of scripts, she decided to wait for three consecutive days during which he said all of the scripts before introducing the next fading step.

Some children master each successive set of scripts more quickly than the prior set. Others say four of five scripts only after extensive prompting and behavioral rehearsals, and it may be appropriate to accept that performance level and allow them to move on to new language tasks, rather than to wait for perfect performances that delay the introduction of new language models. Like everything else about scripts and script-fading procedures, these decisions must be individualized, and are best made on the basis of data on a young person's scripted and unscripted conversation.

10 Scripts for Beginning Readers

One of our first investigations of written scripts focused on three preschoolers, David, Ben, and Jeremiah, ages five, four, and four (Krantz & McClannahan, 1998). These little boys had learned to talk, but they had small vocabularies and usually spoke only in answer to adults' questions or when requesting favorite snacks or toys. Unlike typical children, they never initiated conversation by asking "What's that?" or "See this?" or "Watch me!" They had recently completed a pre-reading program and begun the Edmark Reading Program (1992), and had acquired a few sight words, and they had also learned to use photographic activity schedules. Before the study began, we taught them to read the words "Look" and "Watch me," when those words were randomly presented on flashcards.

The research was conducted in an ordinary classroom that contained preschool-size desks, chairs, and toy shelves, and the students participated one at a time. A photographic activity schedule, presented in a three-ring binder, was displayed on a desk; it contained photographs of play activities such as a toy piano, a coloring book and crayons, a tambourine, and a frame-tray puzzle, and the depicted materials were displayed on shelves and on the floor. Throughout the study, a conversation partner sat nearby, facing the boy. She never asked questions or gave directions, but if the youngster talked to her—about any topic—she responded with short statements about his toys, activities, or topics.

In the first part of the study (baseline), an instructor (standing behind the boy) used graduated guidance to help him open the activity schedule book, point to a photograph, obtain the depicted play materials, engage in the activity, and put materials away. Graduated guidance ensured that the youngster completed this sequence and did not leave the area. Prompts were faded from graduated guidance to spatial fading to shadowing, and finally, to decreased proximity of the instructor to the child. By the end of the baseline condition, each boy had learned to follow the new activity schedule without prompts from the instructor, but it was noteworthy that none of them ever interacted with the conversation partner, although she was a familiar teacher who sat nearby and consistently looked at them.

During the next phase of the research (the teaching condition), the written script "Watch me" was displayed on note cards *above* certain pictures in the activity schedule (such as photographs of throwing a basketball through a preschool-size hoop, or playing a toy piano); and the textual cue "Look" was displayed in the activity schedule *below* other pictures (such as a photograph of a Lego™ block construction, or a coloring book and crayons). The instructor manually guided each boy to point to a script and approach the conversation partner. For example, when the script "Watch me" appeared above a picture of a fireman's hat, the boy was prompted to approach the conversation partner, say the script, and then put the hat on his head. When the script "Look" appeared below a photograph of a chalkboard and chalk, the youngster was prompted to draw on the chalkboard and then point to the script, go to the conversation partner, show his drawing (or scribbles), and say "Look." If a boy did not say the script to the recipient, he was guided to return to the schedule and again point to the textual cue.

Although David and Jeremiah soon learned to approach their conversation partner and say the scripts, Ben often pointed to and read the written scripts in his activity schedule, but failed to say them after he approached his partner. Because it appeared that during his approach he forgot what to say, his scripts were attached to his schedule with Velcro™, we gave him a Velcro bracelet, and the instructor manually guided him to remove a script from his schedule and attach it to his bracelet, so that he could refer to it again after approaching his conversation partner. After eleven sessions with the bracelet, Ben learned to approach and say the scripts to the available adult, and this special procedure was discontinued.

After each boy learned to say the scripts "Look" and "Watch me" without prompts, and after the teacher's proximity was faded to the periphery of the classroom, script fading began. The scripts were faded by cutting away and successively removing one-third, then two-thirds, and then all of the cards on which the scripts were printed (see Figure 10-1). During these fading steps, all three boys continued to say the

Fig. 10-1 Fading the scripts "Look" and "Watch me."

scripts at virtually every opportunity. During the script-fading condition, David said an average of 24 unscripted statements per session, Jeremiah's average was 15, and Ben's was 36. Although David and Ben often said the scripts after they were faded, Jeremiah never again said those words during the remaining sessions.

This research documented that, as a result of scripts and script-fading procedures, the boys displayed impressive new conversation skills. For example, after completing a Sesame Street puzzle, showing it to his conversation partner and saying, "Look," Jeremiah initially imitated his partner's statement—"Big Bird is yellow." But later, after scripts were faded, he combined his scripts with his partner's observations to produce new, unscripted comments such as "Look, yellow bird," "Look, puzzle," and "Yellow two" (while showing a piece of a number puzzle). Similarly, Ben combined the scripts with his interaction partner's comments to achieve novel statements such as "Watch play piano," "Look ball," and "All done."

Fig. 10-2 David approaches a conversation partner, says the script "Watch me," and dons a fireman's hat. His partner replies, "Red hat!"

Fading Pictures and Audiotapes

Although the three preschoolers in our study could read the scripts "Look" and "Watch me," their activity schedules displayed photographs of the toys and activities that became the topics of conversation. Many beginning readers learn to use written scripts more quickly if the scripts are initially paired with photographs and audiotaped cues.

For example, after children learn to use button-activated recorders that are attached to photographs of toys, snacks, and activities, we affix written scripts to Mini-Mes or Voice-Overs (see Figure 10-3). For example, a girl selects a picture of the scooter with Mini-Me and written script attached; she approaches her father, presses the button, and plays the audiotaped script "Scooters are fun." He replies, "You go fast," and waits to see whether she will make any further statements. She says, "Ride scooter" and her father offers the scooter. Or a boy chooses a picture of the jogging trampoline and presses the button on the Voice-Over to play the script, "I like to jump." His teacher says, "You jump on the tramp," he adds "Like tramp," and they move toward the trampoline.

Fig. 10-3 When a child dependably says the script, the photograph is removed; when performance is stable, the Mini-Me is removed, leaving only the written script.

When responding to children's scripted and unscripted statements, parents and teachers model new words that they believe a child understands and that they hope he will use in subsequent conversations. But if the child does not reply after a brief pause, the conversation ends. As noted previously, the child (not the adult) ends the conversation, because extended social interaction may become tiresome and unpleasant.

Initially, teachers and parents manually guide children to point to the words in the scripts as they say them because this helps them attend to the new textual cues; as usual, manual guidance is delivered from behind. When a youngster is dependably saying the scripts, the photographs are removed, leaving only the Mini-Mes and the written scripts. But if a child makes errors, we return to the previous prompt-fading step. In this case, we replace the photographs, and wait until he correctly says the scripts before again removing the pictures.

If a child repeatedly makes errors when photographs are removed, it is often helpful to fade the photographs by gradually cutting away portions of the pictures until the photos are absent. It may also be useful to schedule a separate activity, at a different time of day, to teach a child to read individual words in the scripts when they are presented on flashcards. When the pictures are absent and a child continues to say the scripts, the button-activated recorders are removed. Now the youngster is using written scripts that are easier to construct, readily transportable, and less likely to generate unwanted attention in community settings.

Talk Books

Because it is important for children to try out their emerging conversation skills with different people and in different places, we sometimes create "talk books." A talk book is a three-ring binder; each page contains the text "Talk to ____ about ____." The youngster fills in the blanks by selecting photographs of the people to whom she will talk, as well as photographs of the conversation topics. Photographs that depict topics of conversation are attached to audio cards, and written scripts appear on the cards. On the first page of her talk book, a girl may choose a photograph of a classroom aide who is working at the other end of the room and a picture of animal puppets. She takes her talk book to the other area, approaches the aide, and then removes the topic card, and plays and says the audiotaped script, "I play with puppets." The adult responds "You have a cat puppet." The child may add, "Have a dog," and the conversation partner may say, "Yes, the dog puppet is brown."

Barry, age seven, was especially interested in the alphabet. When he used a talk book at home, he often chose a picture of his mother and a picture of his alphabet book (attached to an audio card) to complete the blanks in the text "Talk to ____ about ____." He approached his mother, played the audiotaped script "I like letters" and said the script. She replied, "A is for apple," and he said, "B is for bird." In a subsequent conversation, he said the unscripted sentence, "C is for cow," a statement he often heard when she read the book to him. After many interactions about the alphabet, Barry often made unscripted statements that his mother had modeled in previous conversations. For example, he said, "B is for banana," "Cow starts with C," and "B is for Barney." He was beginning to learn about social interaction by listening to what others said during their conversations with him.

As noted earlier, when a beginning reader correctly says the scripts, the photographs are removed, so that only the written scripts remain. The words on the audio cards (or voice recorders) are faded next. For example, after the photographs were removed from his foam board, six-year-old Holden's written scripts were fastened to Mini-Mes that were located on or near toys and learning materials that he regularly used. A Mini-Me and the script "Dad reads to me" was attached to the cover of one of his favorite books; "Here's a train puzzle" was attached to a corner of the puzzle; "Can you cut?" was mounted on a plastic box that contained scissors and worksheets with shapes to be cut out; "Do you like cars?" appeared on the side of the toy garage; and "I can count" was affixed to a box of numeral flashcards and plastic counters. Initially, the complete scripts were recorded on the Mini-Mes and Holden quickly learned to repeat them. Next, the words on the audiotapes were successively

How to Create a Talk Book

1. Obtain a three-ring binder and some plastic page protectors. Put black construction paper in each page protector.
2. On each page of the binder, attach the text "Talk to ______ about ______. Leave lots of space for photographs and audio cards that will fill in the blanks.
3. Buy some foam board or get a large piece of cardboard. Pictures and audio cards will be mounted on this board.
4. Take photographs of the people who are available for conversation (for example, Mom, Dad, older siblings, and relatives or family friends who visit frequently), and put the photos in baseball card holders.
5. Take photographs of objects or activities that will be the topics of conversation (e.g., the family pet, a favorite food, the youngster's tricycle or bicycle, a family car, the grocery store) and put them in baseball card holders.
6. Record scripts on audio cards (for example, "I play ball with Duke," "Brownies are my favorite," "My bike is blue," "Dad drives the Honda," and "We shop at Acme").
7. Write the corresponding script on each audio card and attach the relevant photograph to each card.
8. Put Velcro hooks on the back of baseball card holders, and put Velcro loops on the foam board.
9. Attach photographs of people to one half of the foam board; attach audio cards and topic photographs to the other half of the board.
10. Children select photographs of conversation partners from one side of the foam board, and photographs of conversation topics from the other side of the board, mount these in the talk book, seek out the selected partner, and play and say the script.
11. Use the familiar prompting procedures to help children learn to use talk books.
12. When a youngster correctly says a script, remove the accompanying photograph.
13. Fade the words on audio cards from end to beginning, one word at a time.
14. Fade the written scripts from end to beginning, one word at a time.
15. Scripts are absent—only blank audio cards remain.
16. Remove the audio cards.

faded (e.g., "Here's a train," "Here's a," and "Here's") and then the Mini-Mes no longer played the scripts. Subsequently, the Mini-Mes were removed, and only the written scripts appeared on his materials and toys. Finally, the written scripts were faded from end to beginning, one word at a time.

When the scripts were absent and only the cards remained, Holden often combined parts of different scripts to produce new statements such as "I can cut" and "Do you like puzzles?" He also used words that were modeled by adults during prior conversations; for example, "Do you like red cars?" and "Here's a train engine." On the first occasion that he said "Here's an engine" he was holding a caboose. His teacher said, "That's a nice caboose. Here's the engine—toot, toot!"

What to Do When Conversation Fails

Holden said many unscripted statements and questions after his written scripts were faded, but when his teacher removed the cards on which his scripts had appeared, he stopped talking about those topics. That wasn't surprising because at the time, we estimated that he had a spoken vocabulary of less than one hundred words and our data showed that he had a sight-word reading repertoire of twenty-six words. With the scripts completely faded, Holden was as about as effective conversing with his teacher as she might have been if she had attempted to talk shop with a nuclear physicist.

Children's conversation, like ours, is limited to the words they have learned. When we enroll in additional college courses, embark on new careers, start new hobbies, or travel to foreign countries, our interaction with others is often compromised until our vocabularies expand. These experiences are not unlike the experiences of young people with autism.

When Holden stopped talking after his written scripts were faded, his teacher used the recommended error-correction procedure: She returned to the prior prompt-fading step and replaced the blank cards on which his scripts were once written. When the blank cards reappeared, Holden picked up his earlier conversation where he left it, giving the teacher more opportunities to model new language. And his teacher did something else that was very important—she introduced a new set of written scripts that offered more opportunities to learn new conversational language.

11 Scripts for More Accomplished Readers

By "more accomplished" readers, we mean children who read at or above the first-grade level. But a cautionary note is in order: Although children may decode text, they may not comprehend the words they read. Scripts are less effective in building conversation skills if they include many words that children do not understand.

Scripts about Past and Future Activities

We increase the likelihood that children will comprehend conversation when we write scripts that refer to their usual activities. Most of us include discussion of past, current, and future activities in our day-to-day conversation. But many young people with autism are unable to discuss events that are temporally remote—that is, events that happened last year, last month, last week, or even yesterday. We can help them recall and discuss past events if we begin with events that happened a few minutes ago, then an hour ago, then a few hours ago, then early today, and then yesterday or the day before (Krantz, Zalenski, Hall, Fenske, & McClannahan, 1981).

Initially, we write scripts that refer to events that will happen momentarily, and events that concluded only moments ago. For example, the word "talk" or a photograph of a boy talking to someone may appear in his photographic or written activity schedule before and after selected activities. When he encounters this cue, he is guided to obtain a written script from a container on his desk, approach an instructor, and say the script. Scripts that a student might say *before* beginning the next activity are: "Time for math," "I'll get reading," "Let's do spelling," "Gym is next," and "Writing is fun." Scripts that he might use *after* completing those activities are: "I finished math," "All done reading," "We did spelling," "Basketball is great," and "Writing is over."

In these examples, all ten scripts are comprised of three words; longer scripts are introduced as a child acquires more conversational language and more sight-word reading skills. When a youngster says these scripts, his conversation partner might respond with statements such as "I like math," "You read about Sam and Ann," "You can spell 'shoe'," "We'll go outside," "You write your name," and similarly brief replies that are likely to be understood. And if the child makes unscripted statements, his interaction partner follows his lead if possible, or comments on related topics.

When all of the scripts are faded and a youngster continues to talk about math, reading, spelling, gym, and handwriting, we write ten new scripts that will be used before and after five new activities (for example, telling time, playing a video game, counting money, eating lunch, and using a computer), and we place the word "talk" in his activity schedule before and after each of these activities.

After a student completes two sets of scripts about what he is about to do and what he has just done, we insert the word "talk" in his schedule before and after five activities that have never been associated with scripts. If he does not discuss these activities, a new set of ten scripts is introduced. If he initiates conversation about these activities in the absence of scripts, the "talk" cue temporarily remains in his activity schedule, but we occasionally remove it and observe whether he continues to converse with his teachers. When he interacts in the absence of the "talk" cue, it is permanently removed from his schedule.

The next scripts may pertain to events that occurred earlier in the day (the bus ride to school or a morning snack) or that will occur later the same day (lunch or an afternoon bike ride). After young people learn to discuss activities that happened several hours earlier or that will occur several hours later, scripts are developed to help them talk to their parents about events of the school day, and talk to their teachers about things that happened at home the previous afternoon or evening. That is, teachers write one or more scripts about the day's activities, help students rehearse these conversations at school, and send the scripts home at the end of the day. A textual cue in a youngster's home activity schedule, such as "Tell Mom about school," may prompt a student to say the script; or in the absence of a home activity schedule, a parent may use the prompts and prompt-fading procedures discussed in Chapter 6 to teach a child to obtain a script from his book bag and talk about an event of his day.

Parents write scripts about things that happened at home and help their child rehearse them before departing for school, so that the student and his teachers can converse about his home activities. Some youngsters successfully use scripts that differ from day to day. Scripts are not faded in the manner previously described—instead, yesterday's script is discarded and a new one is written. Occasionally, a parent or teacher tests the child's conversation skills by omitting a script for a few days, and the youngster's conversation partner notes whether he discusses events that happened in the other setting. Some parents open conversations by asking, "What happened in school today?" If this does not cue the student to obtain and say the script, parents use the familiar prompting and prompt-fading procedures.

For some children, scripts that change daily are too challenging. We give them scripts about home and school events that happen each day, such as "I played with my sister" or "I typed on the computer." Such scripts continue to be sent to home or school each day until a youngster dependably says them, after which they are faded from last word to first word. When a script is completely faded and a child says the script or says an unscripted statement, a new script is introduced. Many youngsters who first use these "standard" scripts later use scripts that change from day to day.

Photo Albums and Scrapbooks

Scripts used in conjunction with photo albums and scrapbooks help children learn about longer conversational exchanges. Many youngsters enjoy looking at photographs of family members, teachers, and preferred activities. We mount one photograph on each page, and write a script about each photograph. Initially, the child is manually guided to point to a picture, point to the script at the bottom of the page, and orient toward her conversation partner. Usually, the prompt-fading sequence (graduated guidance, spatial fading, and shadowing) is quickly completed if children have had prior experience with scripts and script fading.

A first photo album might contain five to ten scripts such as "This is Mom," "Here's my brother Theo," "Dad is mowing grass," "I like to swim," and "We had a cook out." After each page is turned and the youngster says a script, the conversation partner makes a brief comment ("Mom has a red dress," "Theo is a big boy," "Dad has nice flowers," "There's a ball in the pool," or "I like hot dogs") and looks expectantly at the child. If she makes an unscripted statement, the partner again responds and waits. If the youngster says nothing for ten seconds, she is manually guided to turn the page, or if the prompt-fading sequence has been successfully completed, the conversation partner may say, "I wonder what's on the next page" or "I like to see your pictures" or "I'll turn the page." Scripts are faded in the usual way, from end to beginning, and then a new album is introduced.

Home photo albums offer opportunities for children to learn to talk about important family events. Heather's parents created an album about family milestones. Photographs were accompanied by scripts such as "We went to Disney World," "David has a new house," "Jared is my nephew," "Grandpa bought a tractor," and "My brother got married." After she learned to use the album to engage in conversation with her parents, she also enjoyed showing the pictures and interacting with grandparents, aunts and uncles, and family friends.

If children enjoy drawing, coloring, finger painting, or creating computer graphics, scrapbooks may be created to display their artwork, together with scripts such as "I made a tree," "The sun is yellow," or "This is Uncle Cyril." Many youngsters enjoy looking at the albums and we often invite them to show their prior or current albums or scrapbooks to visitors or others with whom they are not acquainted. Opportunities to interact with new partners help to promote generalization of conversation skills across persons. Similarly, scrapbooks mastered at school can be sent home, to program generalization of social interaction skills across settings.

Using the Telephone

Parents often wish that their child with autism could talk on the telephone, at least briefly, with aunts and uncles or grandparents who live in other parts of the country. Many children do not respond when receivers are held near their ears, but scripts can help to address this problem.

But before they engage in telephone conversation, many young people need some preliminary instruction because they do not appear to know that a voice heard on the telephone represents a conversation partner. Therefore, with parents' input, we write some first telephone scripts, or take photographs of conversation topics that are accompanied by recorded scripts such as "How are you?" "I can spell," and "I like computers." At first, these scripts are said to an instructor who holds a receiver to her ear, stands face-to-face with the student, and replies to each scripted statement. Cell phones or walkie talkies are useful during these practices. After the learner consistently says the scripts, the instructor gradually moves farther away and then moves around a corner and out of sight, but if an error occurs she returns to a location where she is visible to the student.

After a youngster dependably says the scripts when his conversation partner is not visible, he is ready to receive a phone call from a relative. A parent or teacher stands near him and if necessary, uses graduated guidance or spatial fading to help him point to a written script or photograph or play an audiotaped script. Of course, the recipient of the child's phone call probably does not know about script-fading procedures and may ask questions or introduce unfamiliar topics. If the child does not respond, the nearby parent or teacher does not use verbal prompts, but merely guides him to say the next script. Initial phone calls are most successful when the aunt, uncle, or grandparent has a copy of the scripts or a general understanding of what the youngster will say. Family members who review initial scripts and who know a bit about a young person's language-development programs can sometimes better appreciate his hurdles and his growing conversation skills. And as usual, after the initial telephone scripts are faded, new sets are introduced.

More about Fading Written Scripts

In Chapter 10, we noted that scripts that are comprised of only one or two words may be faded by cutting away pieces of the cards on which they are written (see Figure 10-1). But when a child begins to use longer written scripts, we fade them by deleting the last word, then the next-to-last word, and so on.

A Convenient Way to Fade Written Scripts

When scripts are only two or three words in length, it isn't difficult to make a different version of each script for each fading step. The script "Stilts are fun" requires only four separate pieces of paper—three that read "Stilts are fun," "Stilts are," and "Stilts," and a fourth that is blank. If the script is faded to "Stilts" and the youngster makes an error, we can reintroduce the previous script, "Stilts are," and if yet another error occurs, we provide the original script. But when children begin to use longer scripts, it can be rather unwieldy to manage five or six versions of each script. A set of five scripts, each of which is six words in length, requires thirty different script cards and a level of effort that soon becomes burdensome. But it is important to return to a prior script-fading step when an error occurs, because this prevents additional errors.

One solution to this problem is to construct plastic cases that slide forward or backward to cover or reveal the words in scripts (see Figure 11-1). Small plastic envelopes (insert sizes 2⅝ by 3¼ inches and 2¼ by 3½ inches) are available in many stationery stores. A script is placed in the larger plastic envelope, and a blank piece of paper is inserted into the smaller. The smaller envelope can slide in either direction to show or conceal words, and a small binder clip helps prevent its accidental movement.

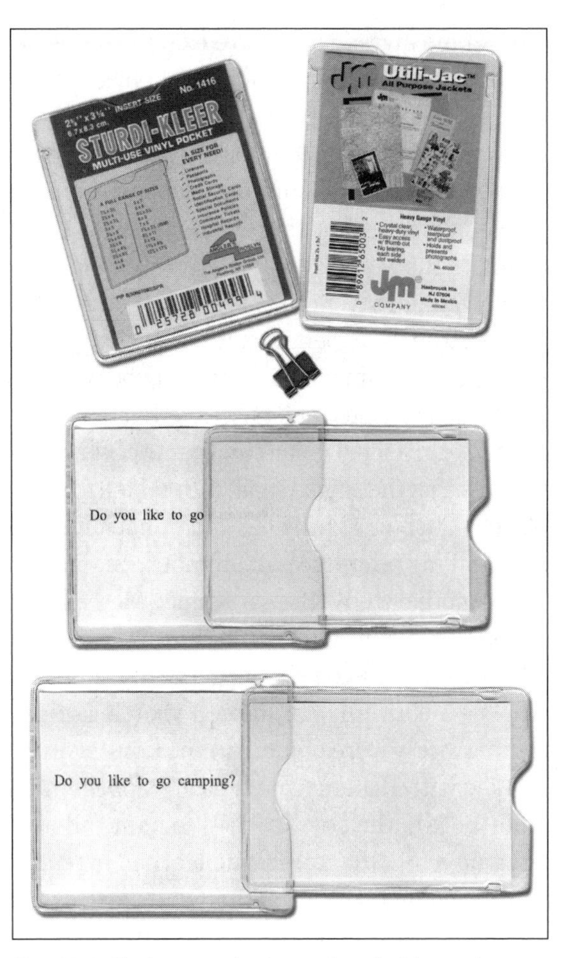

Fig. 11-1 Placing one plastic envelope inside another makes it easy to take the next fading step or return to the prior fading step if a youngster makes an error.

Using Objects to Evoke Conversation

Of course, the goal of scripts and script fading is to enable young people to spontaneously initiate and pursue interaction with others in the absence of audiotaped or written scripts. Ultimately, we want objects, events, and people to evoke conversation.

Some investigators have examined special script-fading procedures that help children talk about objects in their environments. In one study (Sarokoff, Taylor, & Poulson, 2001), snacks and video game cases were placed on letter-sized paper; the first words of the scripts ("embedded textual stimuli") appeared on the snack wrappers or video game cases, and the remaining words appeared on the paper. For example, the words "Gummi Savers" on the candy package began the script "Gummi Savers are my favorite," and the words "are my favorite" appeared on the paper. After the scripts were faded and only the snack packages and game cases remained, the two boys with autism, ages 8 and 9, made scripted and unscripted statements to one another. When they were given new snack and game packages that displayed embedded text that they could read, they talked to each other about the new objects. Chapter 13 provides additional information about how to use script-fading procedures to promote peer interaction.

Another study (Brown, Krantz, McClannahan, & Poulson, 2003) assessed procedures to teach three boys with autism, ages 7, 9, and 13, to engage in conversation during shopping trips. Three mock stores—a convenience store, a sporting goods store, and a video rental store—were created in the boys' school, and each store was stocked with 18 items that typically appear in such stores. Before the study began, the boys learned to name all of the items that would later appear in the stores, and learned to read the individual words (displayed on flashcards) that were later used in scripts.

Nine of the items in each store were associated with scripts and nine were never accompanied by scripts. Scripts were printed on clear adhesive labels that were attached to half of the items in each store. In the convenience store, for example, the script attached to a package of Mini Oreo Cookies was "Little cookies are neat," and the script attached to Reese's Peanut Butter Cups was "Peanut butter is good," but no scripts were attached to Nutter Butter cookies or to a Mounds candy bar. In the video store, some videos were accompanied by scripts (the script about *Antz* was "This movie is about bugs") but other videos, such as *The Lion King,* had no scripts. And similarly, in the sporting goods store, the script attached to a baseball glove was "I love to play catch," but no script was attached to the baseball bat.

The script-fading procedures used in this study were different from those previously described (see box), and were designed to blur the differences between objects that were associated with scripts and items to which scripts were never attached. This is important because, without such special procedures, some children talk when scripts or portions of scripts are present, but do not talk when scripts are absent.

As scripts about convenience store, video store, and sporting goods store were faded, the boys' unscripted statements increased, and in addition, all three of them talked about the items to which scripts were never attached. A post-test showed that their conversation skills generalized to real stores in the community!

Script-Fading Steps *(Brown, Krantz, McClannahan & Poulson, 2003)*

Script-fading sequence for the nine scripts in each mock store:

1. The last word of each script was removed.
2. The last two words were removed.
3. Only the first word of each script remained.
4. Only the first word remained on 6 items, and there were no scripts on the remaining 3 items.
5. Only the first word remained on 3 items, and there were no scripts on the remaining 6 items.
6. Only the first word remained on 1 item, and there were no scripts on the remaining 8 items.
7. There were no scripts.

Don't Forget Rewards!

Rewards for conversation are just as important for older children as for toddlers and preschoolers, and just as important to readers as to nonreaders. When we taught David, Jeremiah, and Ben to initiate conversation by saying "Look" and "Watch me," each boy chose a preferred toy or activity that was delivered as soon as he completed his activity schedule and the session ended. In addition, many of the activities in the schedule were selected because the boys appeared to enjoy them.

When young people use scripts to talk about past and future activities, or to discuss a photo album, or to talk on the telephone, it is important that they earn tokens or other rewards when they say the scripts as well as when they say unscripted statements. In fact, parents and teachers are often so happy and excited about children's novel statements that they immediately deliver several tokens. And because social interaction is difficult, it is a good idea to help children exchange tokens for back-up rewards immediately after conversation ends.

The three boys who learned to talk about the items in a convenience store, a video rental store, and a sporting goods store (Brown, Krantz, McClannahan, & Poulson, 2003) were rewarded with points on single-bank mechanical counters (see Appendix I). Counters were attached to belt loops on the boys' pants, and the instructor also had a counter. The instructor intermittently clicked his counter to reward a boy for saying scripted or unscripted statements. When a youngster heard the click, he advanced his own counter (this skill was taught prior to the study, using the familiar prompt-fading sequence, beginning with graduated guidance and ending with decreased proximity of the instructor to the child). Immediately after each shopping session, the students exchanged points on their counters for preferred snacks.

It is probably less important *how* we deliver rewards (e.g., by dropping snacks in a cup, putting tokens on a token board, or cueing a child to advance a mechanical counter) and more important that we remember to deliver them frequently and immediately after children engage in unprompted conversation. Social interaction tasks are some of the most difficult activities we ask young people with autism to undertake. Like them, we don't enjoy our attempts to accomplish difficult new tasks (such as computer use, in-line skating, learning a foreign language, or learning to prepare a difficult recipe) unless others praise, applaud, and otherwise reward our efforts. Chapter 16 offers additional guidance on choosing and using rewards.

12 Measuring More Complex Conversation

As children become more proficient at using scripts and engaging in conversation, it is important to continue collecting data and measuring their progress. The data provide valuable information about when to lengthen scripts and when to fade them.

After using scripts and script-fading procedures in research and intervention for several years, we developed new definitions of interaction that more accurately represented the children's expanding conversational repertoires (McClannahan, MacDuff, Fenske, & Krantz, 1999). These definitions are tempered by our belief that concerns about grammar should not be permitted to interfere with children's experiences with conversation. We include these definitions here to enable parents and teachers to continue to measure young people's progress when their conversations are longer and more complex.

Defining Interaction

For youngsters who have now developed some conversation skills, *interaction* is defined as understandable statements or questions that:

1. include a noun or pronoun and a verb;
2. are unprompted by another person; and
3. are directed to a recipient by using her name or by orienting toward her while standing within three feet of her.

If a young person makes a statement or asks a question and immediately repeats the statement or question, those repetitions are not scored as interaction. Also, repetition of a conversation partner's statements are not counted as interaction.

Types of Interaction

Scripted interaction is defined as verbal productions that match the most recently used written or recorded script or portion of a script, with the exceptions that:

1. conjunctions, articles, prepositions, and pronouns can be altered;
2. verb tense can be changed;
3. singular or plural word endings can be altered; and
4. a conversation partner's name can be added.

These qualifications are necessary because many young people whose conversational skills are improving have not yet acquired correct syntax and make many grammatical errors. For example, if the script is "I have an iMac computer," a student may say "I have *a* iMac computer." If the script is "Do you go to the movies?" a child may ask "*Did* you go *in* the movies?" And if the script is "Do you like ice cream?" a youngster may query, "Do you *likes* ice cream?" Many young typical children also make such errors, and we do not want concerns about the structure of language to erode children's opportunities to participate in social interaction.

Unscripted interaction is defined as statements or questions that differ from recorded or written scripts by more than conjunctions, articles, prepositions, pronouns, plural endings, changes in verb tense, or a recipient's name. In practice, when young people say the scripts after they are completely faded, those statements are scored as unscripted; but in research, they are scored as a second type of scripted interaction (cf. Stevenson, Krantz, & McClannahan, 2000) because that results in a more conservative measure of unscripted conversation.

During children's early conversations, it is easy to write each of their unscripted words, phrases, or sentences, word by word. But as sentences lengthen and conversation expands, it is increasingly difficult to record everything the youngsters say, and it is necessary to revise the measurement procedures. We continue to score whether a young person says each script or portion of a script, but instead of attempting to write every word of every unscripted statement, we now tally the number of unscripted statements and questions.

These measurement procedures were used with Abby, age twelve. She had previously learned to talk about recently completed and future activities, and was learning to use scripts to engage in telephone conversation. She had completed forty sets of written scripts, and her scripts had gradually lengthened to sentences and questions of four to seven words. She had first-grade reading skills and it was often necessary to teach some of the words on flashcards before new sets of scripts were introduced, but she typically mastered the new words in a few days. Figure 12-1 shows Abby's scripts for Sets 37 through 40. Like most of us, Abby had some favorite topics, one of which was food, and her teacher acknowledged this special interest by creating scripts on that theme. Abby used a written activity schedule that she typed on the computer and printed each morning, and she selected the order of activities in her daily school schedule. The word "talk" in her schedule cued her to obtain a script, approach an instructor, and initiate conversation.

Fig. 12-1 Abby's Scripts for Sets 37 through 40

Set 37
We went to Disney World on vacation.
I went on great rides.
It was a long drive to Florida.
The animal park was really cool.
I saw Mickey Mouse in a restaurant.

Set 38
We ride the train to New York.
The restaurants in New York are great.
My grandparents live in Queens.
I play checkers with grandpa.
Grandma likes to play the piano.

Set 39
What is your favorite restaurant?
I like to go to Burger King.
Mom likes to eat at Red Lobster.
What do you make for dinner?
Do you bake cakes?

Set 40
I make my school lunch every day.
Sometimes I make sandwiches for Dad.
Salads are great on hot days.
Lean Cuisine meals are pretty good.
What did you bring for lunch today?

The data sheet in Figure 12-2 shows that on July 1, 2004, Abby was on fading-step two—the last two words of the scripts in Set 40 were absent. On this day, she said four of the five partially faded scripts. When she did not correctly say, "Sometimes I make sandwiches for Dad," her teacher revealed one more word of that script (see Chapter 11) and that enabled her to say the entire sentence. Prior data on her acquisition of conversation skills suggested that after only one day on which she correctly said all of her scripts, she should advance to the next fading step; this enabled her to complete sets relatively quickly and move on to new sets.

Fig. 12-2 Data Sheet

Sample data sheet for a child who uses sentences. (A blank Data Sheet is in Appendix I.)

Child: *Abby* **Observer:** *Moriah* **Date:** *7/1/05* **Script Set:** *40* **Fading Step:** *2*

Script	Said Script	Number of Unscripted Statements
I make my school lunch every day.	+	//
Sometimes I make sandwiches for Dad.	-	/
Salads are great on hot days.	+	/////
Lean Cuisine meals are pretty good.	+	//
What did you bring for lunch today?	+	///
	N= *4*	N= *13*

Fading Steps:
1 Last words of scripts faded
2 Last two words of scripts faded
3 All but first two words of scripts faded
4 All but first words of scripts faded
5 Script cards are blank
6 Script cards are absent

Figure 12-2 also indicates that on July 1, Abby said thirteen unscripted utterances in five interaction opportunities. Abby's usual teacher collected the data shown in Figure 12-2, but another instructor also observed and collected data on the same day. He also marked

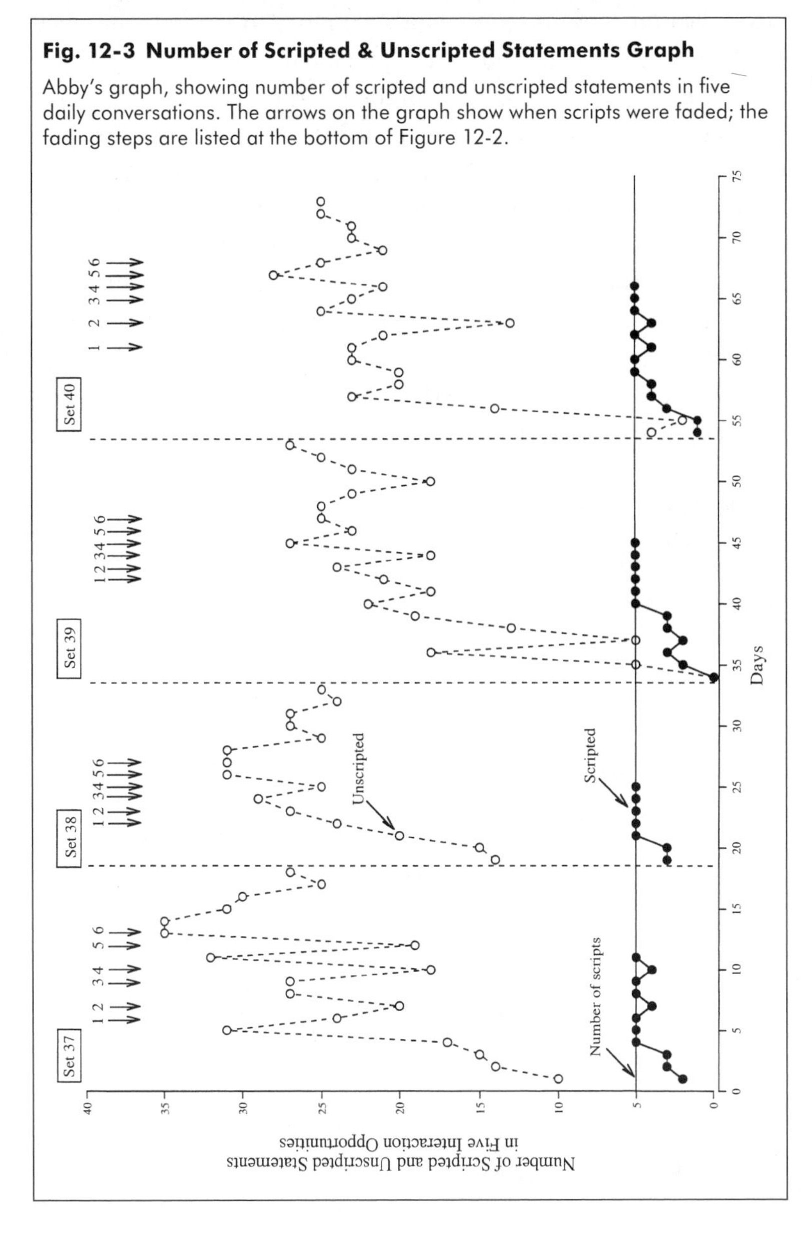

Fig. 12-3 Number of Scripted & Unscripted Statements Graph

Abby's graph, showing number of scripted and unscripted statements in five daily conversations. The arrows on the graph show when scripts were faded; the fading steps are listed at the bottom of Figure 12-2.

minus (-) for the second script and plus (+) for the other scripts. And he tallied a total of fifteen unscripted statements or questions. The two observers calculated their percentage of agreement on unscripted statements by dividing the smaller total (13) by the larger total (15) to obtain .866; this number was rounded to .87 and multiplied by 100 to obtain an interobserver agreement score of 87%.

The graph in Figure 12-3 on the previous page shows Abby's scripted and unscripted statements in five conversation opportunities that occurred on school days when she said the scripts in Sets 37 through 40. She learned to say the new scripts in Set 38 in only three days, but it was six days before she said all of the scripts in Set 40. After she learned to say the scripts, they were rapidly faded, and when scripts and script cards were gone, she continued to talk with her instructors.

It is noteworthy that the final fading step in each set was followed by at least five days without scripts—Abby's teacher wanted her to learn to talk to others without using textual cues. But then the next set of scripts was introduced to help her learn new topics and broaden her conversation.

13 Using Scripts to Promote Peer Interaction

It is not accidental that we teach children to interact with adults before we teach them to talk to other children. Parents and teachers are usually willing and sympathetic conversation partners, but children's responses to each other are much more erratic. Youngsters with autism may ignore one another's initiations, and siblings and typical peers may tease or make nonsensical replies. For these reasons, we strongly recommend beginning peer interaction programs only after children have learned such fundamental skills as approaching and orienting toward adult partners and saying scripts.

Initial peer conversations often focus on preferred toys and activities. For example, a button-activated recorder is attached to a photograph of a peer. A preschooler finds the depicted youngster, presses the button to play a recorded script, and repeats a script such as "Want to race?" or "Want a snack?" or "Let's watch TV." If the peer partner is also a child with autism, he may activate a Mini-Me or Voice-Over that plays a response such as "Yes" or "Okay," after which both youngsters engage in the activity.

Such brief exchanges are gradually embedded in additional activities, with different peers, and at different times of day. A Mini-Me on the door to the playground displays an attached script "I can swing"; a girl says the script to her peer, who activates another Mini-Me and replies with the script "I like to slide." A boy opens his lunchbox, finds a Mini-Me and a written script inside the lid, and says the script, "I have a sandwich." His lunch partner uses his own script to respond, "I have chips." If peer partners are children with autism, both receive similar instruction. If the child with autism will interact with a typical peer, we may initially ask the peer to wait until his friend is finished talking before he talks.

At first, we adults need to identify the topics of peer conversation. For example, young children with autism may talk to one another while constructing a toy car. Each child has a few pieces of the toy, and they use recorded scripts such as "Put wheel on," or "Here's the door," while assembling the toy. Or the pieces of a frame-tray puzzle may be divided between two youngsters, who say scripts such as "This is an apple," or "Look, a banana," while putting the pieces in place.

Pictures may also designate topics of conversation. Figure 13-1 shows Mark and Peter, both age ten, talking about photographs that are displayed in transparent plastic sign holders. Both boys saw the same

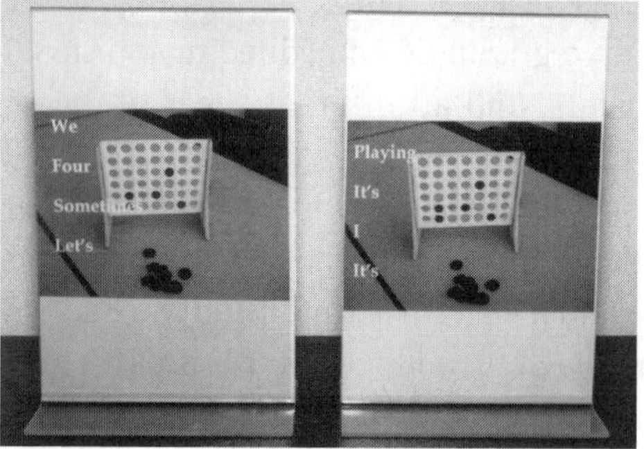

Fig. 13-1 Mark and Peter talk about cars, shopping trips, and games. They both see the same photograph (which is displayed on both sides of a plastic holder), but they have different scripts. Scripts for the game Connect Four have been faded; only one word of each script remains.

picture, but they had different scripts, which were printed on clear adhesive labels and attached to the photographs. The scripts about a Connect Four game are faded to first words. Later, when the scripts were absent, the boys continued to discuss games, cars, and family shopping trips (Fenske, MacDuff, Krantz, & McClannahan, 2003).

Peer conversation is taught with the same prompt-fading and script-fading procedures discussed in previous chapters, but it is worthy of mention that adult prompters often find peer interaction between children with autism more exacting than adult-child conversation because it is necessary to prompt both youngsters.

Preparing for Peer Interaction

1. Select a peer partner for the child with autism.
    a. If the partner is a youngster with autism, he or she should already have learned to approach an adult partner and say an audiotaped script or read a written script.
    b. If the partner is a typical peer, he or she should be capable of following directions such as "Wait for Johnny to talk before you say something to him," or "You use these toys and let Johnny use those."
2. Select scripts that are of interest to both children (for example, "Do you want a cookie?" "Yes, I want an Oreo™").
3. Begin with one conversational exchange—one child initiates and the other responds. When they master one brief exchange, lengthen the interaction.
4. If a youngster uses written scripts in conversations with adults, provide written scripts for peer interaction.
5. Card readers may be used for table-top activities, but Mini-Mes and Voice-Overs are often more convenient for floor play.
6. If both peers are children with autism, identify two adult prompters—one for each child.
7. If the peer partner is a typical youngster, role play the interaction with her, so that she will learn the sequence of statements in the conversation, and will be familiar with the activity or the play materials.

Peer Tutoring

As children's interaction skills expand, peer tutoring often proves useful in promoting conversation. Imagine two preschoolers with autism seated at a little table, facing one another. The boy playing the role of student has Mr. Potato Head™ in front of him, and his partner, who is presently the "teacher," has a card reader and audio cards, to which are attached photographs of Mr. Potato Head's eyes, ears, nose, mouth, and arms. The "teacher" plays an audio card and repeats the script "eyes"; the "student" finds the eyes and puts them on Mr. Potato Head's face (with graduated guidance, if necessary). The "teacher" then plays a card with an attached picture of a pretzel, says the script "Good," and drops a pretzel in a cup near the "student." After Mr. Potato Head is completed and the "student" and "teacher" have consumed the pretzels, the youngsters exchange roles and repeat the activity. There are two key elements in this scenario: First, because the scripts are resequenced each day, the "student" does not know which response to make unless he attends to his peer who is playing the role of teacher; and second, the shared rewards (in this case, pretzels) are available only after both children complete the interaction tasks. If necessary, the adult prompter uses manual guidance to ensure that the snack is not consumed until peer interaction ends.

Typically, during children's first peer-tutoring experiences, it is necessary to assign an adult prompter to stand behind each child. Later, after youngsters learn more about peer interaction, one adult may prompt both "teacher" and "student," but this sometimes requires rapid footwork, because prompts must continue to be delivered from *behind* the learners. Children's contrasting experiences with adult and peer conversation partners often create the likelihood that when response requirements are ambiguous, they attempt to abandon peer partners and engage in the easier task of talking to adults. If they are allowed to do so, development of peer-interaction skills is delayed.

Children who have acquired more expressive language sometimes tutor one another on previously mastered tasks. For example, the tutor displays a picture of a doctor and reads the script, "Who is this?" and the "student" responds "It's a doctor." A three-ring binder is folded back to form an easel and is placed between the two children. When the tutor turns a page, a photograph is visible to the student and the tutor views written scripts on the back of the student's next photograph. If the student's answer is correct, the tutor reads the script "Good" and drops a piece of popcorn (or other preferred snack) into a cup near the student. If the answer is incorrect, the tutor reads the script "It's a doctor. Who is this?" and waits for his peer to respond. The tutor must attend to his peer's responses in order to know whether to praise or correct. If he praises when he should correct, or vice versa, the prompter guides him to point to the other script. Of course, both youngsters play the roles of tutor and student.

Later, young people may tutor one another on not-yet-mastered topics, such as calendar skills, coins, or math facts. For example, the tutor shows flashcards that display addition problems. The side of the card visible to the student presents a problem such as "6 + 3 = " and the side visible to the tutor displays the script "What is __" and the same problem, but the answer is covered by a removable sticker, to prevent the tutor from reading the answer to the student. After the student responds, the tutor removes the sticker and reveals the answer. If his peer's response was correct, he praises him and delivers a token reward; if it was incorrect, he reads the problem and the answer ("6 + 3 = 9") and again asks "What is 6 + 3?" The familiar prompt-fading sequence is used to teach both tutor and student the relevant responses.

After children learn the peer-tutoring format, they may also learn to make varied praise statements. The tutor is given a written list, such as "Right," "Great," "Good for you," "Terrific," "Correct," and "Awesome." A token is placed near each praise statement; when the student provides a correct answer, the tutor says a praise statement and gives him a token. The absence of a token beside a written praise statement cues the tutor to use the next statement on the list. Later, the tutor's script "What is __?" and the praise scripts are faded.

In our experience, many youngsters with autism totally ignore their peers until they engage in scripted peer interaction that results in shared rewards (e.g., using a see-saw, sharing a ride in a wagon, or sharing special snacks). It is important to note that neither participant in these conversational exchanges can complete interaction tasks without attending to the behavior of the other.

Interaction with Siblings

Because peer interaction is challenging, we often teach these skills first in the preschool or school, and then help parents introduce them at home. Preschoolers with autism may learn to play board games such as Barnyard Bingo™ or Candyland™ with a sibling, using scripts such as "Let's play Candyland," "I'll be red," "My turn," "Your turn," and "Good play." If a child says "My turn" when it is not his turn, or says "I'll be red" and then picks up a blue playing piece, he is prompted to use the correct script or select the correct piece. Using graduated guidance and the previously described prompt-fading procedures, we teach youngsters with autism to help themselves to the contents of a nearby bowl of popcorn, peanuts, pretzels, or pieces of rice cake after completing each turn.

Activities are usually explained to siblings in advance. It may also be helpful to teach young siblings to play the game with parents before they begin to play with a brother or sister with autism, and parents may provide further instruction during initial games. Of course, siblings do not need scripts, but they may need to be encouraged to wait for the child with autism to talk, and to reply to his initiations. The presence of snacks often enhances young brothers' and sisters' interest in the games.

Older children with autism may use longer scripts to talk to siblings while playing checkers, bingo, or card games such as Uno™. And sometimes, siblings who are approaching adolescence enjoy making scrapbooks and (with help) adding scripts that enable a brother or sister with autism to talk to them about topics such as popular music, sports, or vehicles.

Peer Interaction in Groups

Scripts and script-fading procedures have been successful in enabling preschool and school-age children to engage in unscripted conversation during meals. Lunch-time conversations for preschoolers often begin with a few photographs attached to button-activated recorders, enabling children to say brief scripts ("Want a cracker?") and share preferred snacks. As speech expands, longer scripts ("What do you have?" "Do you like celery?") are introduced and faded. Eventually, mealtime scripts begin to shift from food to other topics, but this requires careful programming, not only because food may be a preferred subject, but also because it is a visually available cue during meals.

When children begin to engage in unscripted lunch conversation, we support their early efforts by introducing new stimuli that serve as topics for continued peer interaction. Placing unexpected objects on the lunch table often promotes novel conversation; we have added different condiments, unfamiliar fruits and juices, unexpected desserts, and table-top toys. We recommend adding new stimuli frequently. We have been surprised and pleased about the unscripted peer interaction that occurs when toy animals, toy vehicles, novel pictures or books, or unfamiliar utensils are placed on lunch tables.

We have previously noted the importance of avoiding verbal prompts, but that caution deserves repeating because when a young person with autism makes a perfectly good scripted or unscripted statement to a peer and the peer does not respond, we adults usually feel that we should *do something*. But jumping into a peer interaction and verbally prompting the child who is the recipient to "Say ____" often produces conversation that remains one-sided. We adults really have only a few options:

1. Let the conversation partners work it out (which is what usually happens in "real life");
2. manually guide the silent peer to orient (or approach and orient) toward the speaker; or,

3. on the next occasion, give the unresponsive conversation partner a written or recorded script, so that he can respond to his peer without verbal prompts from an adult.

Thirteen-year-old Bryce used written scripts to engage in lunchtime conversation with three other students who had disparate language skills. His recent scripts pertained to family vacations ("We went to Maine"); holidays ("Mom will bake pumpkin pie"); birthdays ("Nathan wants video games"); chores ("I unload the dishwasher"); and hobbies ("My brother plays the drums"). Scripts were placed in plastic containers at each youngster's place at the table, and an instructor intermittently delivered tokens to Bryce and his peers when they said unscripted sentences or asked unscripted questions.

The data showed that often, after scripts were faded, Bryce stopped talking to his lunch partners. For that reason, we interspersed days when he had scripts or partially faded scripts with days when scripts and script cards were absent. The data in Figure 13-2 show that he rapidly learned to say new sets of scripts, which were then faded; but he also made many unscripted statements when there were no scripts. Alternating days when scripts were present and absent helped him learn to talk to his schoolmates when scripts were not available, and each new set of scripts helped him acquire additional subject matter for future conversations. We recently observed Bryce on a day when he had no scripts. He made sixty-eight unscripted statements on topics such as cooking, music, animals, arithmetic, and the foods in his lunch.

In an early investigation of the use of scripts to promote peer interaction (Krantz & McClannahan, 1993), four young people, ages 9 to 12, used written scripts during art activities; a variety of snacks was available during the sessions. As the scripts were faded and unscripted initiations increased, we noticed that some of the students' talk took on the characteristics of teasing: One boy who often attempted to end conversation by saying "Don't talk" or "I don't want to talk" became the recipient of a large number of questions from his peers. And although another boy's requests for snacks

Fig. 13-2 Number of Scripted and Unscripted Statements

Bryce's graph shows the number of scripted and unscripted statements he made during the first twenty minutes of his school lunch with three peers. Open circles show the number of unscripted statements he said when scripts, portions of scripts, or blank script cards were present; triangles show the number of unscripted statements when scripts and script cards were absent. The arrows at the top of the graph indicate fading steps, which were the same as those shown in Figure 12-2.

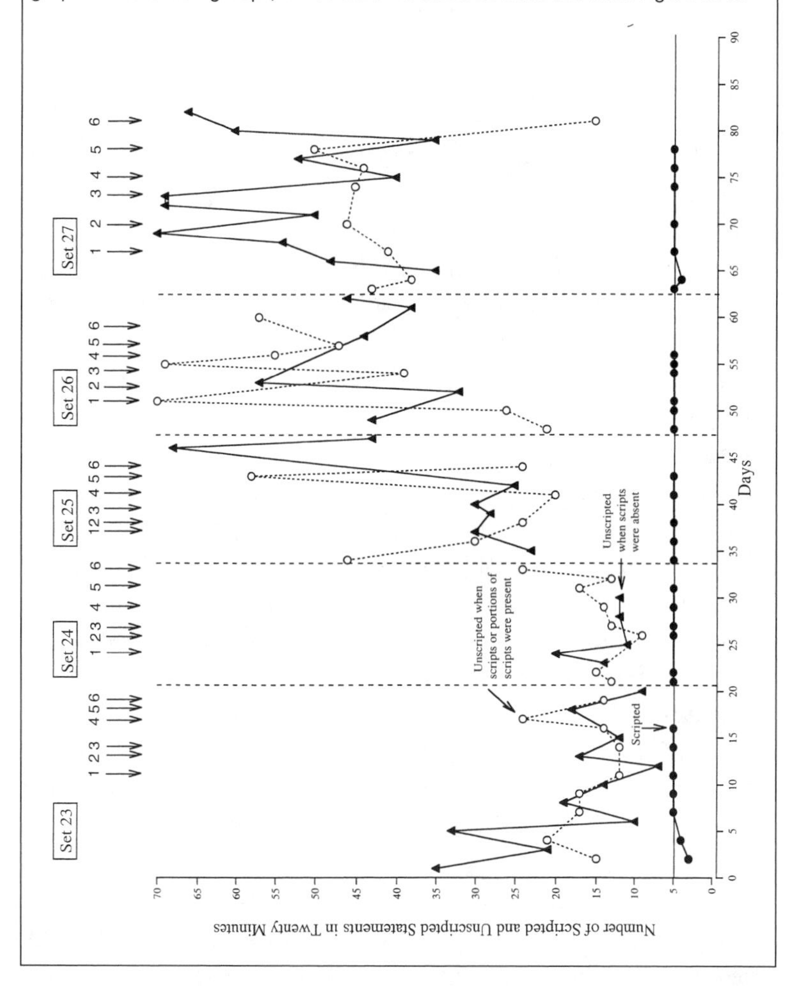

became increasingly specific ("I want a big salt and vinegar potato chip"), his peers often gave him treats that he did not prefer.

Since then, we have continued to observe that when youngsters learn to talk to other children, they may also learn to tease them. We appreciate this added dimension of interaction, because it resembles some of the conversational content of their nondisabled peers. If we are diligent in using script-fading and prompt-fading procedures and in rewarding children's efforts, they learn to pursue conversation under less-than-ideal conditions.

Kurt

After his parents enrolled him in the early intervention program at twenty-two months of age, Kurt made rapid progress. He learned to look at others and to appropriately play with toys; his repetitive movements diminished, and he began to say words and then phrases. His first phrases consisted of the words "here," "see," and "want," combined with nouns such as "book," "bubbles," and "cookie." Later, he learned to say "help me," "can't reach," and "open, please." He mastered many sets of recorded scripts, and used both card reader and button-activated recorders.

By age three, he was speaking in short sentences ("I have a __," "I see a __," "I'm eating/drinking/playing/swinging/coloring") and asking questions such as "What's that?" and "Can I see?" He identified some colors, shapes, numbers, and alphabet letters, and often initiated conversation with adults—but he ignored other children. Standardized tests administered when he was three years, six months of age indicated that his language and pre-academic skills were comparable to those of other three-year-olds, but because of his peer-interaction deficits, his parents and instructors were reluctant to place him in a regular preschool. Instead, they identified an intermediate step to help him learn to talk to other children.

During the summer, daily "play dates" were arranged for Kurt and three typical preschoolers. His instructors planned their daily schedule, which included outdoor play, art, snack time, and music. They also created audiotaped scripts for each activity, and placed audio cards, attached to photographs, in a three-ring binder. During outdoor play, a card reader was placed on a picnic table in the playground, and Kurt's scripts enabled him to approach other children and ask questions such as "Can you climb high? and "Do you like to slide?" and "Do you go to the park?" In art, sample scripts were "I like to color," "Can you paste?" and "Do you like to draw?" and some scripts for snack time were "I like pizza," and "Do you like juice?" We noted that his new friends initially appeared quite interested in his scripts but soon seemed to take them for granted.

Although Kurt was an accomplished user of scripts, his instructors initially found it necessary to manually guide him to approach and orient toward other children, but by the end of the first week the instructors' prompts were faded and script fading began. Kurt's "play dates" continued five days per week for four weeks; three sets of scripts were introduced and faded. In the fourth week he had no scripts, but he continued to approach his peers and say the now-absent scripts as well as many unscripted statements. One month later, he began to attend a regular preschool, with gradually diminishing support from intervention personnel. He now attends preschool without any special assistance, and his parents report that he is an accepted member of his peer group.

14 Teaching Young People to Create Their Own Scripts

In an ideal world, after many sets of scripts have been introduced and faded, young people with autism spontaneously initiate conversation with adults and peers—and often this actually happens! As described in Chapter 13, Kurt learned to talk to adults, and later, to peers in the absence of scripts, and we know many other children who have achieved similar milestones.

Remember Bryce, who stopped talking to his peers after lunchtime scripts were faded? His unscripted peer interaction increased when we alternately provided scripts and removed them (see Figure 13-2).

Anne, now twenty-five and in supported employment, no longer uses scripts; she initiates conversation with her parents, coworkers, work supervisors, peers, and job coaches. Her parents and job coaches don't worry about grammatical errors or disjunctions between topics, but when she occasionally says something that doesn't "make sense" or that is obviously false, they try to respond as they would in any other conversation. They may say "I don't understand," or "I think that __," or "I wonder if that means __."

Using Topic Lists

Not everyone who uses scripts is easily parted from them. We often need special strategies to help young people abandon scripts and launch spontaneous conversation. Learners who have completed many sets of scripts and who have some reading skills may next learn to use topic lists that are based on previous scripts to help them initiate conversation. Some students are taught (with manual guidance and prompt-fading procedures) to check off topics listed on a piece of paper or in a daytimer after they talk about them; this helps them avoid repetitive conversation. But a possible disadvantage of teaching people to check off topics is that they may stop initiating conversation after all of the listed topics have been discussed.

Figure 14-1 shows a topic list and two fading steps. In the first fading step, the last two letters of each word are faded, and in the second step, only the first letter of each word remains. Then there are blanks that are not accompanied by letters, then there is a blank piece of paper, and finally, there is no paper, or no list in a daytimer or appointment book. If the data show that a student's unscripted comments and questions decrease when words in the topic list are faded, it may be helpful to fade one letter at a time. Then instructors or parents must choose whether to allow the shortest words (e.g., pets) to disappear while letters in longer words remain, or whether to retain the first letters of all words until even the longest words have been reduced to single letters. These decisions are best made with reference to the data on unscripted responses. If the number of unscripted statements or questions decreases after a fading step is executed, and does not recover after a few days, it may be important to fade textual cues more slowly.

Writing Their Own Scripts

Unfortunately, teaching some young people to write and say their own comments isn't as simple as fading a topic list. At age 12, Geo used written scripts, said many unscripted statements, and carried on rather lengthy conversations until he reached the final fading step when the blank note cards disappeared. Then his communications markedly decreased. When he arrived at the word "talk" in his activity schedule, he approached an adult and used

Fig. 14-1 A Topic List and Two Fading Steps

Topic List

___Travel
___Weather
___Cooking
___Grandpa
___Pets
___Biking
___School
___Football
___Music
___Restaurants
___Laundry
___Videos

Fading Step 1— *Last two letters faded*	Fading Step 2— *All but first letters faded*
___Trav	___T
___Weath	___W
___Cooki	___C
___Grand	___G
___Pe	___P
___Biki	___B
___Scho	___S
___Footba	___F
___Mus	___M
___Restauran	___R
___Laund	___L
___Vide	___V

a few time-worn sentences to initiate conversation, and he often ended interaction after two or three brief exchanges.

A container with five blank note cards was placed on his desk, and he was given a list of twenty scripts that were commensurate with his reading and handwriting skills. Sample scripts on the list were "Lunch is at 11:30," "I like to swim," "Do you have a cat?" "We play ball outside," "My brother likes Game Boy," "When is your birthday?" "Mom makes cookies," and "It's fun to skate." At first, when he arrived at the "talk" cue in his schedule, he was manually guided to copy a script onto a note card and then cross it off the list, and approach and interact with a teacher. The scripts were frequently re-sequenced to decrease the likelihood that they would be used in the same order day after day.

When Geo's teacher manually guided him to select a script, she allowed his hand to hover over the list and waited for him to choose a sentence or question by putting his pencil on it. Initially, it was necessary to guide him to point to the first word of a script, write that word on the note card, point to the second word and write it on the note card, and so on. But after a few days, graduated guidance was replaced by spatial fading, then the teacher shadowed his movements, and then she moved away from his desk, and he independently selected scripts from the list, copied them on note cards, and approached adults and initiated conversation.

When the data showed that Geo was consistently writing and saying the scripts without prompts, the last words were faded, leaving multipurpose "sentence starters" (e.g., "Lunch is," "I like," "Do you," "We play," "My brother," "When is," "Mom makes," and "It's fun"). These generic scripts remained available for several months. During that time, Geo was rewarded with extra tokens whenever he wrote and said sentences and questions that differed from the original scripts. Then the scripts were completely faded and the list was removed, leaving only the blank note cards on his desk.

We assumed that he would continue to write novel sentences and questions on the note cards. We were wrong! After several days when graduated guidance was necessary to help him write words on blank note cards, the first words of his scripts were returned to his note cards—and he resumed writing his own scripts. A few weeks later, the words on the note cards were gradually deleted. First two note cards were blank, then three, then four, and then five, and he continued to write his own scripts.

But this wasn't the end of the story. The presence of an interested listener did not yet cue Geo to initiate conversation. He never wrote scripts and approached conversation partners unless he encountered the "talk" cue in his activity schedule. On the basis of our experience with other youngsters, we removed all of the "talk" cues in his schedule but left the five blank cards on his desk. When the end of the school day approached and it was time to "clean up" and depart, if he had not written scripts and interacted with others, he was prompted to write something and find a conversation partner. Scripts were hastily written and conversations quickly conducted, with surreptitious glances toward other students who were gathering coats and backpacks and preparing to board school busses. This scenario was regularly reenacted; he continued to write scripts during the last hectic minutes of the school day.

To spare him these anxious moments, we reviewed his daily schedule and attempted to identify preferred activities, such as listening to music, learning to prepare snacks, using the computer, and completing puzzles. When he chose these activities or encountered them in his schedule, he was manually guided to obtain note cards, write sentences or questions, initiate conversation, and then do the activities. Prompts were quickly faded and his conversations increased in length and complexity. And he often combined his own scripts with his instructors' comments to produce novel statements ("I like Burger King," "When is Thanksgiving?" and "Birthday parties are fun").

And Geo's story continued. His teachers gradually added blank note cards to the container on his desk. Sometimes he identified new activities, wrote scripts, and initiated new topics of conversation, and sometimes his teachers briefly guided him to take a note card and write about activities and events that he previously pursued without comment. He learned the give-and-take of conversation. His comments were sometimes surprising, sometimes ambiguous, sometimes humorous, and sometimes not understandable, but he chose the topics, the occasions for interaction, and his interaction partners.

Some children quickly learn to write their own scripts, and even fade their own textual cues. Teaching them to write conversation openers is only a vehicle for promoting interaction. We care less about the writing than about their social talk; we don't prompt script writing if conversation occurs without it, and we reward talking much more than writing. So it's not unusual that some youngsters who have learned to write their own scripts then stop writing them (there are, after all, no consequences for not writing, unless the young person also stops talking).

Broadening Topics of Conversation

Because of the restricted range of interests of many young people with autism, and because of their deficits in reading others' nonverbal cues, problems sometimes arise when they begin to create their own scripts. Namely, some youngsters choose the same topics again and again.

Within weeks after Harry learned to write his own scripts, he stopped writing them. The blank note cards on his desk were ignored, and he appeared pleased with the discovery that he could select his own times, topics, and interaction partners. But his instructors noticed almost immediately that most of his talk related to two topics—*Star Wars* and *TV Guide*. They modeled other topics of conversation ("I saw a movie about cowboys" or "I like to read magazines about camping"), but Harry often turned the conversation back to his favorite subjects. While he continued to engage others in talk about his favorite themes, written scripts were reintroduced to help him learn to talk about additional topics such as popular music, sports, cars, amusement parks, holidays, and family activities.

When he talked about *Star Wars* and *TV Guide,* his conversation partners were interested, active participants, but they did not deliver any rewards; when he talked about other matters, he received many tokens that were exchanged as soon as interaction ended. Later, after he learned to discuss a greater variety of topics, tokens were delivered less frequently and only at the end of conversations.

Some Suggestions for Broadening Conversation

1. Make use of a young person's preferred topics to build new ones. For example, if his conversation is limited to trains, discuss the dining car and extend the conversation to food, or discuss different destinations and extend the conversation to mountain scenery and desert scenery.
2. Change the topic by saying "I don't read *TV Guide*, but I like to read books about horses." If he returns to a discussion of *TV Guide*, try saying, "We were talking about horses."
3. Change the topic to an enjoyable event that will occur in the near future. For example, say, "It's almost time for lunch (or recess or break)."
4. If she returns to a high-interest topic, hold a token just above her token board to indicate that it may soon be delivered, wait for a statement about a new topic, and then deliver the token. After a reasonable time, if she doesn't shift the conversation, make a closing statement and turn away without delivering the token.
5. Be especially interested and animated when he talks about new topics, and deliver extra rewards.
6. Introduce new sets of scripts on new topics.
7. Don't ignore conversation about the time-worn topics, because ignoring conversation partners is a response we don't want youngsters to imitate.

15 Scripts for Nonreaders and People with Severe Disabilities

Despite our best efforts, not all young people with autism learn to read, but nonreaders can nevertheless acquire conversational competencies. Although they may not benefit from written scripts, most can be successful with recorded scripts. Scripts recorded on audio cards have a special advantage that written scripts do not share: They provide models of the prosody of speech—that is the pitch, intonation, and rhythm.

We investigated audiotaped scripts and script-fading procedures for nonreaders in a study that included four boys ages 10, 12, 13, and 15 (Stevenson, Krantz, & McClannahan, 2000). On a standardized test of language comprehension administered just before the study began, the boys' age-equivalent scores ranged from three to seven years. They had learned to talk, but their speech was typically limited to requests ("May I have juice?"), greetings ("Hi, Dad"), and polite words and phrases ("please" and "thank you"). They responded to adults' questions with phrases or short sentences, but they rarely initiated conversation.

The youths had previously learned to use photographic activity schedules. During the study, photographs of audio cards placed in their schedules cued them to approach a conversation partner who held a card reader and audio cards on a clipboard on her lap, and they were manually guided to play a card and say a script. Sample scripts were "My school is PCDI," "Pete likes to play Nintendo," and "What is your favorite food?" The prompt-fading and script-fading procedures used during the teaching condition were similar to those discussed in previous chapters and were very time-efficient; the boys completed all of the script-fading steps in eight to eleven sessions. Subsequently, when scripts were absent and no prompts were delivered, these four youths, who had rarely initiated interaction with adults, said 15 to 35 unscripted statements per session!

But we learned a painful lesson during this investigation. Because the young people had not learned how to end conversations, we instructed the conversation partner that, after approximately four exchanges with a youngster, she should conclude the conversation with a statement such as "It's been nice talking to you," or "Talk to you later." Unexpectedly, the boys soon began to use these statements to end interaction, usually before four exchanges occurred. We did not know whether they simply imitated talk that their partner modeled, or whether they used these statements to terminate social tasks that were difficult for them. Our immediate solution was to ask the conversation partner to sometimes respond to the boys' closing statements with remarks such as "I thought of something else to tell you." Our longer-term course of action was to caution parents and professionals not to model closing statements too soon, and then to do so very carefully.

Some closing statements are much better than others. Statements such as "Goodbye," "See you later," or "I have to go now" usually do not achieve the desired outcome, because it appears socially inappropriate when a teacher, parent, or youngster says "Goodbye" and then doesn't depart. Conversation has a more natural quality if adults model statements such as "I'm going to get back to work," or "I need to do ____ now," or "I'll talk to you later" or "Thanks for telling me about ____" and then, if necessary, turning away to do a different activity. But we shouldn't introduce *any* closing statements until we have had many conversations with young people, have made every effort to make interaction interesting and fun, and have delivered many rewards for their unscripted exchanges.

Silent Partners

Sometimes, when the final words of audiotaped scripts are faded, social talk disappears. This can happen to readers as well as nonreaders, but it appears more likely to happen to nonreaders, perhaps because some of them have smaller vocabularies. Our first recourse is to return to the previous fading step; we re-introduce the words that remained on the audio card or button-activated recorder, and often children resume conversation. After some number of repetitions of blank audiotapes, prior fading step, and blank audiotapes, some youngsters say the now-faded scripts or say unscripted statements, but others remain silent when the scripts are gone.

The next remedy is to take a fresh look at the words a young person does and does not comprehend, because it's difficult to use words one doesn't understand. Picture cards and photo libraries (e.g., Living and Learning, undated; Silver Lining Multimedia, 2000; Stages Learning Materials, 1997) are helpful in assessing comprehension (see Figure 15-1 on the next page). In discrete-trial sessions, parents or instructors may present pictures of common objects and activities, ask "What's this?" or "What's she doing?" or "Show me the ____," or "Find the ____," reward the learner for attending to the pictures, and score responses as correct or incorrect. The information obtained in this fashion supports the development of scripts that are representative of a young person's current language level. Children need not understand every word of every script—new words are often acquired during conversations—but scripts should include more familiar than unfamiliar nouns and verbs.

What if scripts for older children or teenagers are carefully designed to refer to familiar objects and activities but social interaction nevertheless ceases when scripts are faded? A next option is to attach (or reattach) pictures to audio cards, Mini-Mes, or Voice-Overs, and to place these on or near the objects or activities to which they refer. For example, a Mini-Me that plays a script about laundry may be attached to the laundry basket, a Voice-Over that plays a script about setting the table is placed on top

Figure 15-1 Picture Cards and Photo Libraries

Curriculum	Description	Ordering Info.
Library of Vocabulary Photographs Academic Therapy Publications 20 Commercial Blvd. Novato, CA 94949-6191 $109.00	Each of thirteen groups (e.g., appliances, the body, toiletries, vegetables, fruits, office) contains 47 photographs printed on good card stock with a protective coating.	Telephone 800-422-7249 Fax 888-287-9975 www.AcademicTherapy.com
Picture Noun Cards Stages Learning Materials P.O. Box 27 Chico, CA 95927 $149.99	350 photographs from nine categories (animals, food, vehicles, furniture, clothing, toys, everyday objects, shapes, and colors).	Telephone 888-501-8880 Fax 888-735-7791 www.stageslearning.com
Picture This... Silver Lining Multimedia P.O. Box 544 Peterborough, NH 03458 Professional Edition 89.95 Standard Edition $49.95	This CD for Windows and Macintosh contains thousands of photos that can be printed on any size paper, with or without text.	Telephone 888-777-0876 Fax 888-777-0875 www.silverliningmm.com

of the napkins, or an audio card with the script "I'll get my coat" is attached to the closet door. Audiotaped scripts are faded from last words to first words as usual, then the cards are blank, then the cards are absent, and in the last fading step, the pictures are removed. Many young people respond to these remedies; a few do not. In the latter case, parents and instructors must make a choice: Retain the last recorded words on the audio cards or button-activated recorders, or use pictures to cue interaction.

Pictures as Cues for Conversation

When used as cues for conversation, pictures have special advantages not shared by voice recorders. They are small and easily accessible when placed in notebooks, backpacks, pockets, or purses; they can be easily protected in plastic envelopes or baseball-card holders; they are easily transported across settings; and they are inconspicuous when used in public places. But it is important to note that not all pictures are equal. For some people with autism, icons, line drawings, and computer graphics do not have the same impact as photographs or very representational pictures such as those in the commercially available curricula cited above. It is one thing to see a photograph or life-like rendering of a refrigerator, and it may be an entirely different matter to look at an icon or line drawing of a refrigerator. So if we decide to fade recorded scripts and retain pictures to evoke conversation, we should take a good look at the pictures associated with each set of scripts.

Pictures can promote varied conversation, even for people with very severe language delays. Sometimes, after recorded scripts are faded and only pictures remain, young people's statements are confined to the previously faded scripts; but after many sets of scripts are introduced and faded, unscripted statements may begin to appear. But whether or not they depart from scripts, the young people regularly gain attention by approaching others and beginning conversations and they are not excluded from the interaction patterns that are part of most people's daily lives.

It is often helpful to develop categories of talk that are based on assessment of a person's language comprehension, and then to add more categories and more sets of scripts within categories. Figure 15-2 on the next page shows sets of scripts for a youth with a very severe developmental disability. Each script in a set begins with a different word, scripts are limited to three or four words, and the scripts and associated photographs were chosen because the learner identified most (but not all) of the depicted objects and actions when pictures were presented in discrete-trial sessions and he was asked, "What's this?" or "What is he doing?"

When the boy said all of the scripts in a set and continued to say them after voice recordings were faded and only the pictures remained, a new set was introduced, but the previous set was not discarded. It was retained along with all of the other sets of photo-

Figure 15-2 Photographs and Related Scripts by Category

Category: Morning activities

Set 1

Photograph	Script
Alarm clock	Alarm clock rings.
Bed	I make the bed.
Toothbrush	Brush my teeth.
Shower	Take a shower.
Comb	Comb my hair.

Category: Home-living activities

Set 1

Photograph	Script
Broom	Sweep the floor.
Vacuum	Vacuum the carpet.
Iron	Iron my clothes.
Coat hangers	Hang the shirts.
Dishwasher	Put dishes in dishwasher.

Category: Leisure activities

Set 1

Photograph	Script
Television	I watch television.
Computer	Computer is fun.
Bicycle	Ride the bike.
Puzzle	Do a puzzle.
Music system	Listen to music.

Category: Food

Set 1

Photograph	Script
Pizza	Pizza is great.
Cereal	Eat cereal for breakfast.
Hamburger	Look, it's a hamburger.
Sandwiches	Sandwiches are for lunch.
Milk	I drink milk.

Set 2

Photograph	Script
Carrot sticks	Have carrots for lunch.
Bagels	Put jelly on bagels.
Yogurt	Peach yogurt is good.
Bananas	Mom likes bananas.
Cookies	Do you like cookies?

graphs he had learned to use to initiate conversation. Each day, he not only learned to use the recordings and photographs in a new set, but he also used one of the previously mastered sets. This created additional opportunities for him to talk with others and helped to maintain the statements and questions he had previously acquired.

We know some adults with autism who have learned to enjoy others' attention, but whose small verbal repertoires severely limit their opportunities to initiate and pursue conversation. Recorded scripts and photographs make it possible for them to participate in social talk. At home or in the group home, scripts such as "What's for dinner?" "What are you doing?" and "Where's (family member)?" can launch friendly exchanges. Scripts also enable them to discuss favorite activities. When they initiate using scripts such as "I like baseball," "McDonald's is great," or "On Friday, I see (sibling)," these initiations invite others to share their special interests, model additional language, and include them in conversation.

16 Making It Work

Teaching a young person with autism to talk with us, like most other things we want to teach, involves *behavior shaping*, or rewarding successive approximations to the behavior that we ultimately want him to display. For example, when teaching social interaction skills, we begin by rewarding a child for approaching and looking at adults, and when those responses occur with some regularity, we reward him somewhat less often but we systematically provide rewards each time he says or approximates one-word scripts. And when the youngster dependably says one-word scripts, we intermittently reward him for those responses; but when he says two-word scripts, we follow each of these new approximations to the goal with powerful rewards.

Behavior shaping takes practice. To successfully shape behavior one must:

1. learn to deliver rewards immediately after a target response occurs, and
2. learn not to deliver rewards when a child does not respond or makes responses that are more distant from the goal behavior than his recent responses.

At every step of introducing and fading scripts, parents and teachers must ask whether the response the learner just displayed is at least as good as, or better than the responses he has been making, and, if so, they must provide powerful rewards. When progress is slow or negligible, that may be due to errors in the shaping process.

The types of rewards we deliver also have an impact on the development of social talk. One shouldn't assume that because a youngster requested or appeared to enjoy a certain toy or snack yesterday, she will enjoy it today. In fact, some children's preferences seem to shift from minute to minute. We can solve this problem by teaching them to choose from an array of toys or snacks. Toddlers can learn to express preference by reaching for or pointing to an item when two or three options are presented. Providing a choice just before a child engages in a social interaction task increases the likelihood that the reward we deliver is actually of interest to her.

Early in intervention, it may be necessary to use edible rewards, such as bites of cracker, pretzel, or cookie. Bites must be small, so that they can be quickly consumed. If a youngster receives a big bite of chewy candy when he runs a card through the card reader and is still consuming this treat when he fails to approach an interaction partner, the error is rewarded. And as noted earlier, the prompter should deliver edibles from behind the child by putting small bites into his mouth. We don't want children to look at or attempt to obtain the snacks, because it is not the rewards but the presence of a conversation partner that should come to evoke social interaction.

As children learn to make choices from gradually expanding arrays of toys, snacks, and activities, they should also be taught to earn and exchange tokens for back-up rewards of their choice. Tokens make it possible to adjust the magnitude of rewards. For example, a preschooler who recently began to say some unscripted words and phrases may receive two tokens when he makes an unscripted comment, but one token at the end of a conversation during which he only says a script. Youngsters with autism do not initially find social interaction rewarding; pairing tokens with social talk helps them learn to value conversation. For a more extensive discussion of tokens and other reward systems for children with autism, see *Incentives for Change* (Delmolino & Harris, 2004).

Selecting Scripts

When we develop scripts for young children and people with severe language delays, each script in a set begins with a different word. And as noted earlier, the selection of words in scripts is based on a young person's current language level. The script "I go to the Methodist church" isn't very useful to a youngster who hasn't learned about denominations or theological nuances; the script "I go to church" may be a better choice. The conversation partner can then respond "Mom takes you to church" or "You go to church on Sunday." Scripts should be age-appropriate; a toddler may say the script "I want potty" but a six-year-old should say "Bathroom," or "Bathroom, please," or "May I go to the bathroom?" And scripts should be similar to the things other people say; we don't say "I like to eat chocolate pudding," we say "I like chocolate pudding." Scripts shouldn't sound stilted.

When it's time to construct new sets of scripts, we may ponder whether the learner's preferred activities suggest topics of conversation. When he was a toddler, Martin especially enjoyed playing with Sesame Street stamps that made giggling sounds when ink was applied to paper. After brief audiotaped scripts (e.g., "Here's Ernie) were faded, he said his first unscripted words and phrases. Shayna enjoyed making snacks and often requested opportunities to make microwave popcorn or crackers with cheese spread; when scripts about these activities were introduced, she said more unscripted statements than ever before. Diego's favorite activity was bike riding, and Stella's was watching Disney videos; scripts on these topics produced many unscripted sentences and questions. With support from job coaches, Dean held a position in the grounds maintenance department of a large business; scripts and script-fading procedures helped him learn to discuss his job, but after he learned scripts about his day-off activities, the data showed further increases in unscripted conversation. Creating scripts about young people's favorite pursuits often promotes unscripted interaction.

Should beginning readers use recorded or written scripts? Data on a child's unscripted utterances are helpful in answering this question. For example, does the length or complexity of her unscripted statements exceed her current reading skills? If so, audiotaped scripts may be a better choice. Further, if we are concerned about a youngster's prosody (suppose, for example, that her speech sounds "flat" and mechanical), we may decide to continue the recorded scripts, at least for a while, to provide her with additional models of appropriate inflection, volume, and pronunciation. Or we may continue audiotaped scripts in some activities or settings and introduce written scripts in others.

Modeling Conversation

In an earlier chapter, we noted that the conversation partner should look attentive when a young person is talking, make interesting comments, use words that are likely to be understood, and model appropriate voice volume and inflection. And it is also important to individualize conversation length. When young children are learning to approach and say a speech sound or a one-word script, the adult replies and the interaction ends. After youngsters learn to say words or phrases and begin to make a few unscripted comments, conversation may encompass two exchanges. Subsequently, a child may determine whether or not to extend the dialogue—if he makes another unscripted statement, the adult responds and delivers rewards. Remember, social interaction is a difficult task for people with autism. Chats that are too lengthy may make conversation punishing.

Adult partners do not ask questions or give directions because this transforms the activity from a conversation to a discrete-trial training session with the attendant problems of dependence on verbal prompts. They also avoid echoing a youngster's comments (e.g., "Bubbles *are* fun," or "You *do* shop with Mom"). Such repetitions do not offer new directions for conversation and it is therefore less likely that a young person will reply.

In many instructional activities, we use behavior-descriptive praise (e.g., "Good, you said 'me!'" or "You're right, three plus three *is* six!"), both to confirm that a child's response is correct and to help him understand which response is receiving praise and approval. But behavior-specific praise is not characteristic of ordinary talk. We do not usually say things like "Fantastic, you told me you like to ride your bike" in day-to-day chats with typical children. Behavior-descriptive praise is a valuable teaching tool, but it isn't a good model of commonplace conversation.

In Chapter 15, we recommended not modeling closing statements until young people learn the give-and-take of conversation and learn to participate in conversations that include several exchanges. Typically, children with autism do not seek out conversation partners or extend interaction until many interaction attempts have been rewarded. If closing statements are too quickly modeled, youngsters soon use them to prematurely end conversations. But when it's time to teach them to close conversations, some closing statements are better than others. "'Bye" and "Gotta go" and "See you later" are socially inappropriate when no one goes anywhere; instead, we model multi-purpose statements such as "I'd better get busy," "I'm going to ____ now," "I guess I'll ____," or "I need to finish ____."

Fading Prompts

A key feature of the prompt-fading procedures discussed in Chapter 6 is that when used skillfully, they prevent many errors. The prompt-fading sequence—graduated guidance, spatial fading, shadowing, and then decreasing the adult's proximity to the learner—promotes independent performance and helps young people learn to attend to natural cues for conversation (the availability of a partner, an interesting object or event) rather than to the adult's prompts.

We often notice that it is the last step in the sequence, increasing the distance between the child and the adult, that is likely to be forgotten by parents and teachers. Gradually decreasing adults' proximity is essential, because we want youngsters to learn to actively seek out interaction partners. Teachers should reward students for moving across greater and greater distances and eventually going from one end of the classroom to the other, or from one classroom to another to initiate conversation. Parents should reward children for leaving the family room and coming to the kitchen or laundry room to find them and talk to them.

Programming Generalized Interaction Skills

When first sets of scripts are introduced, most youngsters display their nascent interaction skills only with the instructor or parent who is their usual partner, but the goal is to make conversation skills generalize or transfer from the first partner to other partners. This rarely happens without special programming. At first, the same prompt-fading procedures and the same frequency of rewards are necessary every time a youngster encounters a new partner. Later, parents or teachers observe that fewer prompts are needed, or that some prompts can be faded when new partners are introduced. After learning to talk with many different adults, the young person's conversation skills eventually generalize to new people who have never participated in teaching and who have never rewarded the child for talking to them. If a young person does not initiate interaction with an unfamiliar person, we continue to prompt and reward him for talking to new partners—that is, we continue to program for generalization of conversation skills.

Although a youngster talks to new adult partners, it may not be assumed that he will now talk to new peers. It is necessary to program the transfer of interaction skills to peers by prompting and rewarding him for talking to another peer, and another, and another, until he finally strikes up a conversation with a new peer who wasn't present during conversation training.

Programming the generalization of social interaction skills is central in helping children learn to engage in ordinary conversation. We want them to talk not only to parents, but also to teachers; not only to classmates, but also to siblings; not only to family members, but also to relatives; and not only to relatives, but also to community members such as the priest, the pediatrician, and the barber. And we want them to engage in social talk in different places and at different times—on the playground, in the lunchroom, in the classroom, at grandmother's house, in restaurants, and at church school. These outcomes are achieved when we systematically introduce and fade successive sets of scripts on occasions when children engage in conversation with different people, in different activities and settings, and at different times.

17 Solving Problems

Every parent and instructor we know who has used scripts and script-fading procedures has encountered a few rough spots along the way. We often learn a great deal from these temporary complications. The following paragraphs review some problems and suggested solutions.

He doesn't approach his partner or he approaches but doesn't remain near her.

If a youngster does not accomplish these basic components of social interaction, the prompter returns to manual guidance to ensure his success and rewards prompted responses. After prompt fading begins, only unprompted approaches are rewarded.

She approaches but doesn't orient toward her conversation partner.

The prompter returns to manual guidance and guides the youngster to remain in front of her partner until she orients. If the girl says the script without looking at her partner, the partner does not respond and the youngster continues to be manually guided to remain near her partner. If she does not orient within a designated period of time (e.g., 30 seconds), the prompter conducts a behavioral rehearsal. The audio card and photograph are returned to the youngster's activity schedule, and the entire sequence is repeated. Behavioral rehearsals cease and the youngster is rewarded when she orients toward the adult conversation partner.

He doesn't say recorded scripts.

In separate teaching sessions (not during conversation training), seat the child in front of a card reader and sit behind him. Guide him to play a recorded script and wait for him to imitate. If he doesn't imitate within ten seconds or if he displays off-task behavior, guide him to play the script again, and ask him to repeat it. For example, if the script is "cookie," instruct "Say 'cookie.'" If he does not imitate, conduct a behavioral rehearsal—guide him to play the script and instruct him to repeat it. If he does, reward his imitative response and quickly guide him to run the same card through the machine. Provide immediate and highly preferred rewards for imitating recorded scripts in the absence of your instructions.

If these suggestions are not effective after many practice sessions, return to verbal-imitation training. In the meantime, maintain what he has already learned about interaction; let him initiate conversation by playing audio cards and approaching and orienting toward conversation partners.

She says a script and then echoes my reply.

Verbal-imitation sessions teach youngsters to imitate our verbal models and often children don't discern when they should repeat what we say and when they should not. We can help them learn when to repeat by giving the instruction "Say ____" during language-training activities when we expect them to imitate, and by never giving any instructions when we are teaching conversation.

If a girl initiates and then frequently repeats her partner's comments, we rapidly intervene, because continued practice makes it more difficult to interrupt this pattern and teach alternate responses. When she approaches and says a script, the conversation partner replies and then quickly turns away from her to discourage an echolalic response, and the prompter immediately guides the girl to play another recorded script. After the script is played, the partner turns back and attends to the youngster while she says the script, and again replies and quickly turns away. Of course, echolalic responses are never rewarded, but saying the scripts and saying unscripted utterances are occasions for powerful rewards.

Suppose that a child says the script "Ride bike." The mother replies, "You ride with Dad," and the youngster repeats, "ride with Dad." The parent does not respond to her daughter's repetition, and if she is playing the role of conversation partner and the role of prompter, she quickly steps behind her daughter and guides her to select and play the next script—"Wear helmet." After her daughter says this script, the mother rewards her with a token, responds, "Your helmet is blue," and then rapidly turns away. If the girl does not repeat her comment, the mother delivers more tokens and the conversation ends.

He doesn't read the written script aloud.

If necessary, use graduated guidance to help the youngster pick up a script and hold it in his view while he initiates conversation. Consider having someone stand behind him and guide him to point to each word in a script. If this is not effective, put each word on a separate flashcard and teach them in discrete-trial sessions. Present a flashcard, instruct "Read," and reward correct reading responses. After the child consistently reads the flashcards, stand behind him and guide him to point to a word on a card. If he does not read the word, use the instruction "Read," but reward only those responses that are not accompanied by that instruction. When the youngster dependably reads flashcards without verbal prompts or graduated guidance, return to scripted conversation.

She doesn't say scripts after scripts are faded.

If she now says unscripted words, phrases, or sentences, we celebrate. But if she isn't talking at all, it's important to return to the prior fading step. If she abandoned conversation when the audio card or button-activated recorder disappeared, make them available again. If she stopped talking when confronted with a blank card or a Mini-Me without a message, return to a single word. If the reappearance of a single word is not effective, continue to restore words in scripts until the youngster is successful; then repeat the fading steps. If this strategy doesn't achieve the desired results, create shorter scripts, or provide more opportunities to say the scripts before beginning to fade them.

He doesn't make any unscripted statements after scripts are faded.

Sometimes, children don't continue conversation because their verbal repertoires are so small that they have nothing to say. In this case, introduce more scripts and model more conversation. But sometimes youngsters stop talking because social interaction is not a preferred activity. The first recourse is to offer powerful rewards that are earned by engaging in conversation and that are only available at that time, and to deliver exceptionally large amounts of those rewards for making unscripted statements. For example, if a child especially enjoys Gummy Bears, reserve them as rewards for conversation. When he makes an unscripted comment, give him all of his tokens and let him immediately exchange them for Gummy Bears.

If the data suggest that a young person has enough language to make a few unscripted contributions to conversation, we may select a different alternative: Use graduated guidance to ensure that he remains in close proximity to his partner until he eventually says an appropriate unscripted comment. Then provide powerful rewards and end the conversation.

She perseverates on a single topic.

A first remedy is to teach a variety of comments about the preferred topic. If a girl enjoys talking about Disney World, write many sets of scripts about that topic, and gradually expand the scripts to encompass related topics (e.g., air travel, hotel, amusement park rides, restaurants, family members, Disney characters, Disney movies). Don't leave preferred topics too soon, because they may help to make social interaction rewarding. Gradually introduce scripts about new topics and don't forget to reward novel statements. It is also a good idea to check our own conversational variety. Do we make the same responses day after day, or do we model new comments?

He never again discussed some topics after scripts were faded.

Sometimes we introduce scripts because we want to help a young person add a new dimension to his conversational repertoire—and sometimes these efforts fall flat. The youngster says the scripts until they are completely faded and then never says them again in our presence. Carlos used scripts to respond to scenarios that warranted statements of concern: For example, a teacher or parent reported stubbing her toe, cutting her finger, or having a headache. During the last fading steps, Carlos continued to say, "Does it hurt?" or "Are you okay?" or "I'm sorry," but when fading was complete he no longer responded to extremely obvious enactments of illness and injury. After many more sets of scripts were introduced and successfully faded we returned to scripts about empathy and this time, after scripts were faded, he expressed concern when it was appropriate to do so. When some topics of conversation disappear after scripts are faded, provide more experience with conversation and return to difficult topics at a later time.

The disappearance of conversation related to previous scripts may also indicate that day-to-day interaction does not maintain those subjects. If there was once a Voice-Over near the microwave oven that played the script "I like popcorn," occasionally return to that topic with statements such as "You make popcorn in the microwave" or "You haven't made popcorn lately," and wait for a reply. If scripts about grocery shopping were faded weeks ago, remember to talk about it from time to time. Spontaneous conversation about previously scripted topics is most likely to occur if scripts pertain to recurring activities such as meal preparation, housekeeping tasks, outdoor play, story time, bath time, trips to a fast-food restaurant, or visits to grandparents' homes. We all find it easier to talk about familiar topics than about unfamiliar ones.

Some people don't want to be conversation partners.

Typical peers may be too engrossed in their own activities to talk with the child with autism. Family acquaintances and community members are sometimes uncomfortable about interacting with people with disabilities. Aunts, uncles, cousins, and grandparents are sometimes too busy with their own agendas to stop and talk. Occasionally, all of us encounter social rebuffs and it is probably impossible to protect young people with autism from such experiences, but we can do our best to reward children's conversational efforts, to teach their brothers and sisters to do the same, and to make social interaction fun.

He seems bored with the scripts.

Like everyone else, young people with autism may lose interest in doing the same things over and over again. After the scripts are faded, it's important to introduce new scripts and new topics that help to keep social interaction fresh and interesting.

But children may also appear uninterested in activities that are difficult. Sometimes we also dislike attempting difficult tasks, but after we master them we enjoy displaying our new skills. If we want young people to develop conversational competence, it is important to provide many practice opportunities, use manual guidance and prompt-fading procedures, and deliver powerful rewards for social talk. As social interaction skills develop, children typically appear more interested in social activities, and many even choose them.

He tries to grab rewards before he earns them. Sometimes he flaps his hands, and even tries to hit or bite.

The prompting and prompt-fading procedures described in this book are effective because they prevent and correct errors. If a child flaps his hands or engages in other repetitive behavior, manual guidance corrects that error and prevents additional errors—the prompter quickly guides the youngster to pick up an audio card and move toward the card reader, or to play the audio card and approach the conversation partner.

Many children with autism display response chains in which one inappropriate behavior leads to another. For example, hand flapping is followed by loud vocal noise, then the child jumps or runs, and then he hits or bites others who attempt to interrupt these activities. If we use manual guidance when the youngster flaps his hands, we not only interrupt that behavior, but we may also prevent responses such as vocal noise, jumping, running, hitting, and biting. By conducting behavioral rehearsals and manually guiding children to engage in appropriate responses, such as playing audio cards, pressing buttons on Mini-Mes or Voice-Overs, or approaching conversation partners, we create opportunities to reward and strengthen desirable behavior.

Children progress most rapidly when we provide very clear feedback about their behavior. That is, we immediately deliver tokens, snacks, play materials, or activity rewards when youngsters make correct responses, and we prompt and conduct behavioral rehearsals when they display inappropriate behavior. If we are inconsistent, young people may not acquire social interaction skills, may learn slowly, or may learn responses that we did not intend to teach. For example, if a child does not say a script and we decide that he is tired and needs a break, we may find that next time he is even less likely to initiate conversation.

She makes unscripted statements, but sometimes we can't understand what she is saying.

When children's speech is unintelligible, we adults are often tempted to ask questions ("What did you say?") or give instructions ("Say that again"), but this may turn a social exchange into a discrete-trial teaching session and make children dependent on our verbal prompts. Instead, we may respond as we would in other conversations ("Sorry, I didn't understand that" or "I didn't hear you"). When typical toddlers say things we don't understand, we often guess at their meanings. For example, a toddler says "ba-ba" and the parent replies "Bottle. There's juice in your bottle." We do the same for children with autism; if their comments are unintelligible, we do our best to offer a pleasant, relevant comment. Often, the most recently used script provides some clues about the topic.

He says unscripted comments and asks unscripted questions, but he mispronounces words and uses incorrect grammar.

Many young people with autism have considerable difficulty learning to use pronouns, plurals, and correct verb tense and sentence structure. Of course we want them to learn correct grammar and pronunciation but those skills are best taught at other times, not when we are teaching conversation. Consider how we feel when we are talking about topics of interest to us and someone interrupts and corrects us. When we converse with youngsters with autism, we use correct grammar because we are aware that the language we model often reappears in their later conversation—including our colloquialisms and expletives.

He says things that are out of context and if we change the subject, he doesn't switch to the new topic.

Often, "out of context" statements are a result of children's limited language repertoires. Suppose that an adult says, "You like to play with your farm animals" and the child replies, "I like trains." If the youngster had a larger spoken vocabulary, he might say, "I like trains better than farm animals" or "I'd rather talk about trains" or "Tommy the Tank Engine is my favorite toy" or "I can't think of anything else to say." We address such skill deficits by continuing to provide new scripts that offer more examples of conversation, by constructing sets of scripts so that all of the scripts in a set pertain to a specific topic, and by modeling statements that create conversational contexts ("My favorite toy is ____," "I want to tell you about ____," and "I'm going to ____").

Brett and Seb and Libby...

When Brett entered the Early Intervention Program at 22 months of age, he did not talk. His first sets of one-word scripts were recorded on audio cards, and he learned to run cards through the machine and approach and orient toward a conversation partner. As his verbal repertoire expanded, his scripts gradually changed from words to phrases to sentences. Before his fourth birthday, he completed his last set of scripts (Set 28), said many unscripted statements, and asked many unscripted questions. In the weeks that followed, he initiated conversation with many different people at home and in other settings, discussed a variety of topics, and asked "Why?" with astonishing frequency. At age 4, he began to attend a regular preschool, where he is indistinguishable from his peers.

Seb first learned to use one-word scripts when he was 4. Later, he imitated short phrases recorded on audio cards, and brief comments modeled by his teachers often reappeared in his later conversation, but he seldom initiated conversation in the absence of scripts. When he was ten, scripts and script-fading procedures enabled him to discuss activities that he was about to pursue and activities that he had recently completed, and he carried on conversations about these topics in the absence of scripts. Presently, at age 15, he uses scripts every other school day. On days with no scripts, he seeks out conversation partners and is very talkative; he especially enjoys discussing movies, videotapes, computer games, restaurants, vacations, and dinosaurs. On days when he uses scripts, they are designed to help him learn to discuss additional topics.

When Libby was 12, her receptive language skills were equivalent to those of a 5-year-old, and she had first-grade reading skills. Although she responded to parents' and teachers' questions with phrases and simple sentences, she rarely initiated interaction and when she did, her conversation usually focused on requests for preferred activities. Libby was one of the first participants in our studies of scripts and script-fading, and the data documented that these procedures resulted in substantial increases in her social talk. Presently, at age 22, after many sets of scripts were introduced and faded, she uses a computer to type and print her scripts, and then selects and seeks out conversation partners.

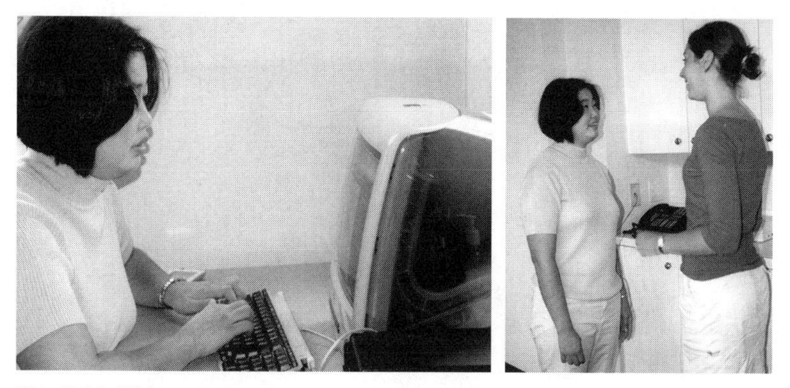

Fig. 17-1 Libby composes some new scripts and prints them, but forgets to take them with her when she talks to a job coach. (She developed her own script-fading procedure.)

Her topics are wide-ranging, her interactions are often lengthy, and we find her an interesting conversationalist. And we notice that, after she types and prints her scripts, she frequently forgets to bring them with her when she approaches conversation partners.

Scripts and script fading procedures have helped many young people with autism learn to interact with others. Some youngsters acquired conversation skills after a few sets of scripts were presented and faded, and some engaged in unscripted interaction only after completing many, many sets of scripts. In any case, our conversations with them are much more satisfactory because they are not controlled by the instruction "Say ____." Their unscripted statements and questions please us, surprise us, amuse us, and sometimes leave *us* speechless.

Appendices

Appendix A Audio Card Readers

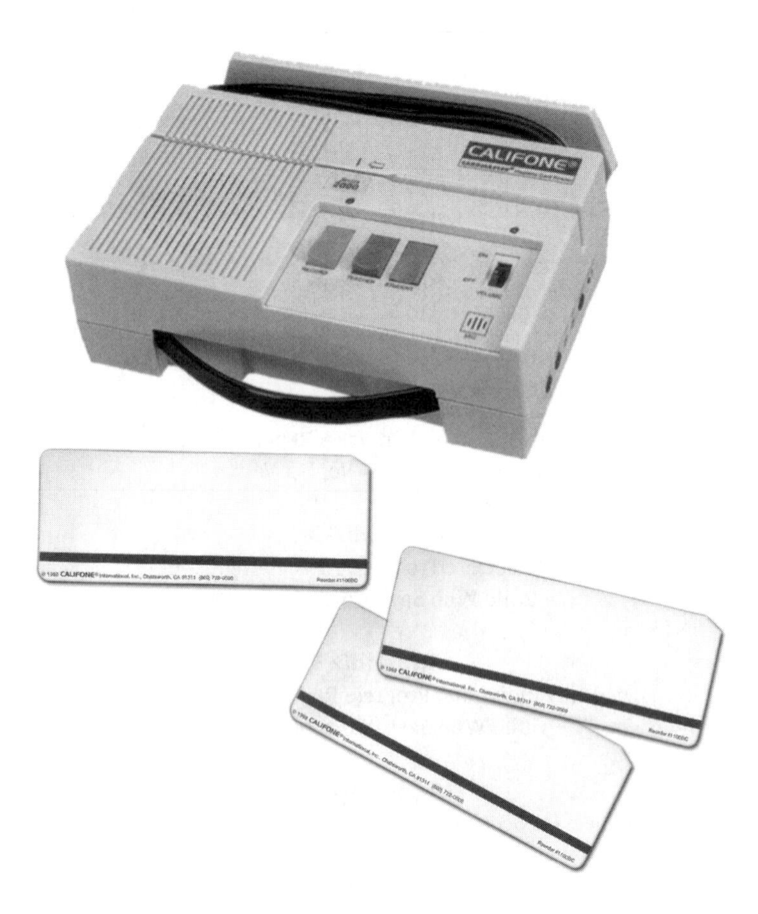

Califone card readers may be ordered from Valiant International Multi-Media Corporation, 55 Ruta Court, South Hackensack, NJ 07606 (Telephone: 800-631-0867, Fax: 201-440-8051). Model VCR-2010 costs $189.00 and 800 blank cards cost $92.00. They may also be ordered from *www.800valiant.com*. Drake audio card readers are available from *www.pcicatalog.com* for approximately the same price.

Appendix B Data Sheet Used to Measure the Progress of a Child Who is Not-Yet-Verbal

Child: ____________ **Observer:** ____________ **Date:** ____________ **Script Set:** ___

Script #	Get card from schedule	Play audiotape	Approaches and orients
1			
2			
3			
4			
5			

Response definitions
[a] Removes audio card from a page of the activity schedule
[b] Runs card through card reader and correctly plays audiotape
[c] Approaches to within 3 feet of conversation partner and orients toward him or her

Script 1 ________________________________

Script 2 ________________________________

Script 3 ________________________________

Script 4 ________________________________

Script 5 ________________________________

Appendix C Daily Individual Progress Report for a Child Who is Not-Yet-Verbal

Child: ______________________ **Correct=** ▒ **Incorrect=** ☐

Script Set: __________

Notes										
5c Orients										
5b Plays audiotape										
5a Gets card										
4c Orients										
4b Plays audiotape										
4a Gets Card										
3c Orients										
3b Plays audiotape										
3a Gets card										
2c Orients										
2b Plays audiotape										
2a Gets Card										
1c Orients										
1b Plays audiotape										
1a Gets card										
Year: Date:										

Response definitions
[a] Removes audio card from a page of the activity schedule
[b] Runs card through card reader and correctly plays audiotape
[c] Approaches to within 3 feet of conversation partner and orients toward him or her

Script 1 ____

Script 2 ____

Script 3 ____

Script 4 ____

Script 5 ____

Appendix D Data Sheet Used to Measure the Progress of a Child Who Says Words or Phrases

Child: ____________ **Observer:** ____________ **Date:** ____________ **Script Set:** __

Script #	Get card from schedule	Play audiotape	Approaches and orients	Says script
1				
2				
3				
4				
5				

Response definitions
[a] Removes audio card from a page of the activity schedule
[b] Runs card through card reader and correctly plays audiotape
[c] Approaches to within 3 feet of conversation partner and orients toward him or her
[d] Says the word or words on the script

Script 1 ____

Script 2 ____

Script 3 ____

Script 4 ____

Script 5 ____

Appendix E Daily Individual Progress Report for a Child Who Says Words or Phrases

Child: ____________________ **Correct=** ▒ **Incorrect=** ☐

Script Set: __________

Notes										
5d Says script										
5c Orients										
5b Plays audiotape										
5a Gets card										
4d Says script										
4c Orients										
4b Plays audiotape										
4a Gets Card										
3d Says script										
3c Orients										
3b Plays audiotape										
3a Gets card										
2d Says script										
2c Orients										
2b Plays audiotape										
2a Gets Card										
1d Says script										
1c Orients										
1b Plays audiotape										
1a Gets card										
Year: Date:										

Response definitions

[a] Removes audio card from a page of the activity schedule

[b] Runs card through card reader and correctly plays audiotape

[c] Approaches to within 3 feet of conversation partner and orients toward him or her

[d] Says the word or words on the script

Script 1 ____

Script 2 ____

Script 3 ____

Script 4 ____

Script 5 ____

Appendix F Sample Data Sheet for Scoring Scripted and Unscripted Interaction

Child: ____________ **Observer:** _______________ **Date:** ___________ **Script Set:** ___

Scripted Interaction	Correct (+)	Incorrect (-)
Script 1:		

Unscripted Interaction

Scripted Interaction	Correct (+)	Incorrect (-)
Script 2:		

Unscripted Interaction

Scripted Interaction	Correct (+)	Incorrect (-)
Script 3:		

Unscripted Interaction

Scripted Interaction	Correct (+)	Incorrect (-)
Script 4:		

Unscripted Interaction

Scripted Interaction	Correct (+)	Incorrect (-)
Script 5:		

Unscripted Interaction

Number of correct scripted statements ______

Number of unscripted statements ______

Appendix G Data Sheet for a Child Who Uses Sentences

Child: ________ **Observer:** ________ **Date:** ________ **Script Set:** ___ **Fading Step:** ___

Script	Said Script	Number of Unscripted Statements
	N= ______________	N= ______________

Fading Steps:

1 Last words of scripts faded

2 Last two words of scripts faded

3 All but first two words of scripts faded

4 All but first words of scripts faded

5 Script cards are blank

Appendix H Button-Activated Voice Recorders

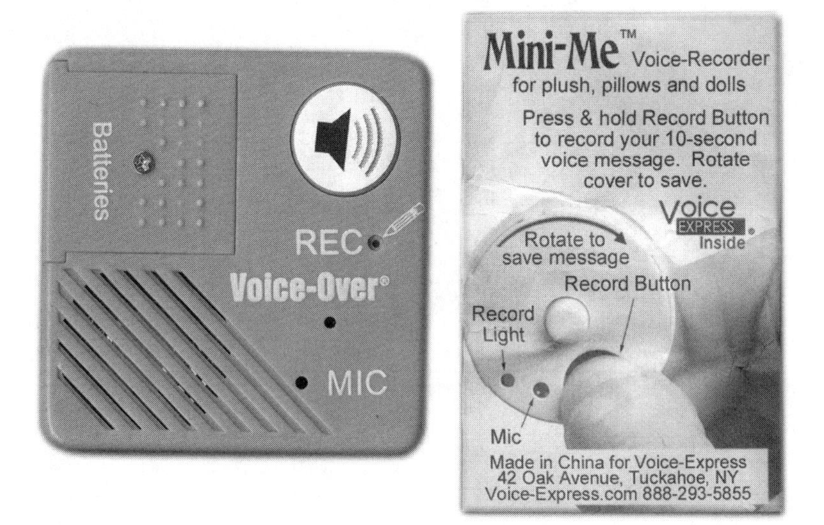

These miniature voice recorders may be ordered from Voice Express Corporation, 42 Oak Avenue, Tuckahoe, NY 10707. Telephone: 888-293-5855 or visit *www.voice-express.com*.

One box of 20 voice recorders costs approximately $80.00; individually recorders cost about $9.00 to $10.00. Mini-Mes are approximately three-fourths inch deep; Voice-Overs are about one-fourth inch deep and are more easily placed in activity schedule books.

Appendix I Hand Counter

Hand counters may be ordered from Fisher Science Education, 485 S. Frontage Road, Burr Ridge, IL 60521 (Telephone: 800-955-1177 or fax orders to 800-955-0740; *www.fishersci.com/education*).

It tallies to 9999 and resets to zero with a push of a button. One mechanical counter costs $10.60.

Appendix J Materials Needed for Script-Fading Programs

- Card reader and audio cards (see Chapter 4 and Appendix A)
- Mini-Me Voice Recorder, Voice-Over, or other button-activated recorders (see Chapter 9 and Appendix H)
- Children's preferred snacks and toys
- Tokens and token boards (small clipboards, plastic discs or coins, and Velcro™ dots that are used to attach tokens to clipboards)
- Data sheets (see Appendices B, C, D, F, and G)
- Progress Report charts and graph paper (see Appendix C, Chapter 7, and Figure 7-2)
- Baseball card holders (available from hobby shops) that are used to attach photographs to audio cards, button-activated recorders, or pages of a child's activity schedule (see Figures 4-1, 4-2, and 9-1)
- Camera and film or digital camera and printer
- Plastic envelopes used to conceal and reveal parts of written scripts and small binder clips (see Figure 11-1)
- Mechanical counters, useful in collecting data on children's unscripted statements (see Appendix I)

References

American Psychiatric Association (1994). *Diagnostic and statistical manual of mental disorders* (4th ed.). Washington, D. C.: Author.

Baer, D. M., Wolf, M. M., & Risley, T. R. (1968). Some current dimensions of applied behavior analysis. *Journal of Applied Behavior Analysis, 1,* 91-97.

Bijou, S. W., & Baer, D. M. (1965). *Child development II: Universal stage of infancy,* p. 171. New York: Appleton-Century-Crofts.

Brown, J. L., Krantz, P. J., McClannahan, L. E., & Poulson, C. L. (2003, May). *Moving toward environmental control of language for children with autism.* Paper presented at the meeting of the Association for Behavior Analysis, San Francisco, CA.

Cooper, J. O. (1987). Stimulus control. In J. O. Cooper, T. E. Heron, & W. L. Heward (Eds.), *Applied behavior analysis* (p. 315). Columbus, OH: Merrill Publishing Co.

Delmolino, L., and Harris, S. (2004). *Incentives for change: Motivating people with autism spectrum disorders to learn and gain independence.* Bethesda, MD: Woodbine House.

Edmark Corporation (1992). *Edmark Reading Program,* 2nd ed. Hiawatha, IA: Riverdeep.

Fenske, E. C., Krantz, P. J., & McClannahan, L. E. (2001). Incidental teaching: A not-discrete-trial teaching procedure. In C. Maurice, G. Green, & R. M. Foxx (Eds.), *Making a difference: Behavioral intervention for autism.* Austin, TX: Pro Ed.

Fenske, E. C., MacDuff, G. S., Krantz, P. J., & McClannahan, L. E. (2003, May). *Teaching children with autism to participate in topic-related peer conversation.* Paper presented at the meeting of the Association for Behavior Analysis, San Francisco, CA.

Hart, B., & Risley, T. R. (1999). *The social world of children learning to talk* (p. 194, pp. 278-279). Baltimore: Paul H. Brookes.

Heward, W. L. (1987). Basic concepts. In J. O. Cooper, T. E. Heron, & W. L. Heward (Eds.), *Applied behavior analysis* (p. 19). Columbus, OH: Merrill Publishing Co.

Krantz, P. J., & McClannahan, L. E. (1993). Teaching children with autism to initiate to peers: Effects of a script-fading procedure. *Journal of Applied Behavior Analysis, 26,* 121-132.

Krantz, P. J., & McClannahan, L. E. (1998). Social interaction skills for children with autism: A script-fading procedure for beginning readers. *Journal of Applied Behavior Analysis, 31,* 191-202.

Krantz, P. J., Zalenski, S., Hall, L. J., Fenske, E. C., & McClannahan, L. E. (1981). Teaching complex language to autistic children. *Analysis and Intervention in Developmental Disabilities, 1,* 259-297.

Living and Learning (undated). *Photo nouns Set 1, Set 2.* Cambridge, England: LDA.

Lovaas, O. I. (2003). *Teaching individuals with developmental delays: Basic intervention techniques.* Austin, TX: Pro Ed.

MacDuff, G. S., Krantz, P. J., & McClannahan, L. E. (2001). Prompts and prompt-fading strategies for people with autism. In C. Maurice, G. Green, & R. M. Foxx (Eds.), *Making a difference: Behavioral intervention for autism* (pp. 37-50). Austin, TX: ProEd.

McClannahan, L. E., & Krantz, P. J. (1997). In search of solutions to prompt dependence: Teaching children with autism to use photographic activity schedules. In D. M. Baer and E. M. Pinkston (Eds.), *Environment and behavior* (pp. 271-278). Boulder, CO: Westview Press.

McClannahan, L. E., & Krantz, P. J. (1999). *Activity schedules for children with autism: Teaching independent behavior.* Bethesda, MD: Woodbine House.

McClannahan, L. E., MacDuff, G. S., Fenske, E. C., & Krantz, P. J. (1999, May). *Building conversational skills for children, youths, and adults with autism: How to use script-fading procedures.* Workshop presented at the meeting of the Association for Behavior Analysis, Chicago, IL.

Pierce, W. D., & Epling, W. F. (1995). *Behavior analysis and learning* (p. 41). Englewood Cliffs, NJ: Prentice Hall.

Sarokoff, R. A., Taylor, B. A., & Poulson, C. L. (2001). Teaching children with autism to engage in conversational exchanges: Script fading with embedded textual stimuli. *Journal of Applied Behavior Analysis, 34,* 81-84.

Silver Lining Multimedia (2000). *Picture this...version 3.0.* Poughkeepsie, NY: Author. (CD-Rom for Windows 95, 98 or NT and Mac OS).

Stages Learning Materials (1997). *Language builder picture cards.* Chico, CA: Author.

Stevenson, C. L., Krantz, P. J., & McClannahan, L. E. (2000). Social interaction skills for children with autism: A script-fading procedure for nonreaders. *Behavioral Interventions, 15,* 1-20.

Sundberg, M. L., & Partington, J. W. (1999). The need for both discrete trial and natural environment language training for children with autism. In P. M. Ghezzi, W. L. Williams, and J. E. Carr (Eds.), *Autism: Behavior-analytic perspectives* (pp. 139-156). Reno, NV: Context Press.

Glossary

Back-up reward. An object (such as a toy or snack) or activity that a child obtains when he exchanges his tokens.

Baseline. During baseline, a teacher or researcher takes repeated measures of the behavior of interest before intervention procedures are introduced. This establishes a criterion against which any changes due to the intervention procedures may be assessed (Pierce & Epling, 1995, p. 41).

Behavioral rehearsal. A parent or teacher immediately helps a child practice responses that were incorrectly performed.

Discrete-trial teaching. The teacher gives an instruction; the student responds or does not respond; if necessary, the teacher prompts to help the student make a correct response; and the teacher delivers a consequence (Lovaas, 2003, p. 62).

Echolalia. Repeating what others say, as if echoing them.

Incidental teaching. The teacher waits for the child to initiate interaction about an object or activity of interest and then asks the child for more elaborate language. After the child responds, the teacher provides the child with the object or activity for which he or she initiated.

Perseveration. To repeatedly say the same words, phrases, or sentences; to return to the same topic again and again.

Prompts. Instructions, gestures, demonstrations, touches, or other things that we do to increase the likelihood that children will make correct responses.

Prompt dependence. A person responds to prompts instead of responding to the cues that are expected to evoke behavior. For example, the person does not greet a person who has just arrived, but depends on a prompt such as "Say 'hello.'"

Reinforcer. A stimulus that follows a behavior and increases the likelihood that the behavior will occur in the future. If a child enjoys yogurt, then providing a bite of yogurt immediately after each occasion when he looks at his mother may increase his visual attending to her. Rewards are reinforcers only if they increase the behavior they follow.

Response. A specific behavior. When using script-fading procedures, we measure responses such as saying the scripts and making statements that are different from the scripts.

Stimulus. An aspect of the environment. "Stimuli are people, places, and things; light, sound, odors, tastes, and textures" (Heward, 1987, p. 19). In this book, some stimuli that are of special interest are scripts and conversation partners.

Target response. A behavior that parents or teachers are attempting to increase or decrease.

Tokens. Initially, tokens (such as happy faces, stickers, plastic discs, or coins) are not reinforcers, but they acquire value when they are repeatedly paired with other reinforcers, such as favorite toys or preferred snacks. Tokens retain their reinforcing properties only if there are regular opportunities to exchange them for back-up rewards. A toddler may earn five tokens and exchange them for a tickle or a jog on her father's knee. A preschooler may earn ten tokens and exchange them for an opportunity to play with a top or ride in a wagon. Tokens are important in autism intervention because they can be delivered immediately to reward children's appropriate performance, they can be used in many different settings (home, school, community), and they prevent rapid satiation.

Verbal-imitation training. An adult models a sound, word, or phrase, and asks the child to imitate the model. For example, the adult says, "Say 'ma,'" and rewards the child for imitating or attempting to imitate. This type of discrete-trial teaching is an important and widely used component of language training for children with autism.

Index

About the Authors

Since 1975, **Drs. Lynn E. McClannahan** and **Patricia J. Krantz** have been the Executive Directors of the Princeton Child Development Institute. Nationally and internationally known, the Institute was one of the first community-based, applied behavior analysis programs in the United States for people with autism. Drs. McClannahan and Krantz have mentored many young professionals who now contribute to the education of students with autism. They are the authors of many journal articles and book chapters, as well as the book, ***Activity Schedules for Children with Autism: Teaching Independent Behavior*** (Woodbine House, 1999). They have made international contributions to autism intervention in Australia, France, Great Britain, Greece, Norway, Russia, and Turkey. Their research on language development, social interaction skills, staff training, and program evaluation has been recognized by the Senate of the State of New Jersey (1988); by the National Teaching-Family Association (1989); by the Norwegian Association for Behavior Analysis (1991); by Division 25 of the American Psychological Association (1994), and by the Society for the Advancement of Behavior Analysis (1999).